The Beginner's Guide

Computer

Systems

Principles, Practices, and Troubleshooting

MARK JOHN P. LADO, MIT

ISBN: 9798308934653

Imprint: Independently published

DEDICATION

This book is dedicated to the passionate learners, aspiring IT professionals, and educators who tirelessly explore the intricate world of computer systems. Your curiosity, perseverance, and commitment to understanding technology drive innovation and progress.

To the mentors and teachers who ignite the spark of knowledge, guiding students toward excellence—your dedication shapes the future of computing.

To the problem solvers and troubleshooters who embrace challenges, ensuring seamless digital experiences for all—your expertise keeps the world connected.

And to my family and loved ones, whose unwavering support and encouragement fuel my journey—this endeavor would not be possible without you.

May this book serve as a valuable resource, inspiring generations to master the principles and practices of computer systems with confidence and passion.

ACKNOWLEDGMENT

The completion of this book would not have been possible without the support, encouragement, and contributions of many individuals.

First and foremost, I extend my heartfelt gratitude to my mentors and educators, whose guidance and expertise have shaped my understanding of computer systems. Your knowledge and insights have been invaluable.

I sincerely thank my colleagues and peers in the field of IT and computer science for their discussions, feedback, and shared experiences, which have enriched the depth of this book.

A special thanks to my family and loved ones for their unwavering support, patience, and encouragement throughout this journey. Your belief in me has been my greatest motivation.

Lastly, to the readers—whether students, professionals, or enthusiasts—may this book serve as a valuable resource in your learning journey.

TABLE OF CONTENTS

This page is intentionally left blank

CHAPTER 1

INTRODUCTION TO

COMPUTER SYSTEMS

A computer system is a multifaceted entity, far exceeding the simple image of a physical machine. It's a synergistic integration of hardware, software, and firmware, each playing a crucial, yet distinct, role in information processing. Hardware encompasses the tangible components, the physical building blocks of the system. This includes the central processing unit (CPU), the "brain" executing instructions; memory (RAM), providing temporary data storage for active processes; storage devices (HDDs, SSDs), ensuring persistent data retention; and peripheral devices like keyboards, mice, and monitors, facilitating user interaction. Software, conversely, comprises the intangible instructions, the programs and data that direct the hardware's operations. This ranges from the operating system (OS), managing system resources and providing a platform for other software (e.g., Windows, macOS, Linux), to application software,

1

designed for specific tasks like word processing (e.g., Microsoft Word, LibreOffice) or web browsing (e.g., Chrome, Firefox). Firmware, often the unsung hero, bridges the gap between hardware and software. It's a low-level software embedded within hardware components, responsible for initialization and basic control. A prominent example is the Basic Input/Output System (BIOS) or its modern counterpart, the Unified Extensible Firmware Interface (UEFI), residing on the motherboard and managing the boot process. This foundational layer ensures the hardware is ready for the operating system to load. A common misconception, particularly among novice users, is the perceived independence of software from hardware. In reality, they exist in a symbiotic relationship. Software is meticulously crafted to execute on specific hardware architectures, leveraging the hardware's capabilities. For instance, software compiled for an ARM processor will not run on an x86-based system. Furthermore, the hardware's limitations, such as processing power and memory capacity, directly influence the complexity and performance of the software it can effectively support. Consider the development of complex simulations or AI models; these require substantial processing power and memory, necessitating specialized hardware like GPUs (Graphics Processing Units) to achieve acceptable performance. This interconnectedness underscores the importance of a holistic understanding of computer systems, acknowledging the dependencies and interactions between these three fundamental components. As Stallings (2018) emphasizes, "Computer organization refers to the attributes of a system visible to a programmer, or those attributes that have a direct impact on the execution of a program," while "Computer architecture refers to those attributes of a system visible to a programmer" (p. 5). This distinction highlights the layered approach to understanding computer systems, from the user-visible software layer down to the intricate hardware details. A deeper understanding of these intricacies allows computer scientists to optimize software for specific hardware, design new hardware architectures to support emerging software paradigms, and ultimately, build more efficient and powerful computing systems.

1.1 TYPES OF COMPUTER SYSTEMS

The world of computer systems presents a remarkable diversity, ranging from the familiar personal computer (PC) to the robust server farms powering the internet and the specialized embedded systems controlling our everyday devices. Personal computers, designed for individual use, cater to a broad spectrum of needs, manifesting in various form factors. Desktops offer a balance of performance and expandability, ideal for resource-intensive tasks like video editing or gaming. Laptops prioritize portability, allowing users to work and play on the go. All-in-ones integrate all components into a single unit, simplifying setup and minimizing clutter. Servers, in contrast, are the workhorses of networked environments. They are engineered for centralized tasks, providing services and resources to multiple clients, be it serving web pages, managing databases, or hosting applications. Their architecture emphasizes high availability, scalability, and robust performance, often featuring redundant components and advanced cooling systems. Mobile devices, including smartphones and tablets, represent a convergence of portability and computing power. These pocket-sized powerhouses offer functionalities comparable to traditional PCs, enabling communication, entertainment, and productivity on the move. Embedded systems, often overlooked, are specialized computers integrated into larger systems to perform dedicated, often real-time, functions. They are the unsung heroes controlling everything from the anti-lock braking system in your car to the intricate mechanisms within industrial machinery. These systems prioritize efficiency, low power consumption, and reliability, often operating under strict constraints. This heterogeneity in computer systems directly reflects the vast array of tasks they perform in our increasingly digital world. A common question, especially for those new to the field, is how to select the appropriate computer system for a given task. This decision is rarely straightforward and depends on a confluence of factors. Processing requirements are paramount; computationally intensive tasks, like scientific simulations or 3D rendering, necessitate systems with powerful CPUs and GPUs. Portability needs are equally important; if mobility is a key factor, laptops or mobile devices become the natural choice. Cost considerations play a significant role; balancing performance with budget constraints is crucial. Furthermore, the specific applications that will be used dictate the necessary hardware and software ecosystem. For example, running specialized engineering software might require a workstation with a high-end graphics card and a large amount of RAM. As Tanenbaum and Bos (2015) discuss, "The choice of a computer system depends on many factors, including cost, performance, size, power consumption, and software availability" (p. 12). Understanding these trade-offs and carefully evaluating the requirements of the intended task are essential for making informed decisions about computer system selection. Moreover, emerging trends like cloud computing and edge computing further complicate this landscape, offering new paradigms for resource allocation and computation. These paradigms require a deeper understanding of distributed systems and network architectures, adding another layer of complexity to the decision-making process.

1.2 Basic Computer Operations

The fundamental operations of a computer system revolve around a cyclical process: input, processing, output, and storage (IPOS). This cycle forms the bedrock of how computers interact with data and instructions. Input involves feeding raw data or commands into the system. This is typically achieved through various input devices, such as keyboards for textual input, mice for pointer-based interaction, touchscreens for direct manipulation, or even more specialized devices like scanners for digitizing documents or microphones for capturing audio. The processing stage, the core of the computer's activity, takes this raw input and manipulates it according to the instructions provided by software. This manipulation occurs within the central processing unit (CPU), the "brain" of the computer. The CPU performs arithmetic calculations (addition, subtraction, multiplication, division), logical operations (comparisons, Boolean logic), and data movement operations, all orchestrated by the software instructions. Output then presents the results of this processing to the user or another system. Common output devices include monitors for visual display, printers for hard copies, speakers for audio output, and network interfaces for transmitting data to other systems. Finally, storage provides a mechanism for preserving data and instructions for later use. This persistence is crucial, as it allows computers to retain information even when powered off. Storage devices encompass a range of technologies, including hard disk drives (HDDs) for traditional magnetic storage, solid-state drives (SSDs) for faster, flash-based storage, and cloud storage for remote, network-accessible storage. Understanding this IPOS cycle is paramount to grasping the fundamental principles of computer operation. It provides a framework for analyzing how data flows through the system and how different components interact. A common point of confusion, especially for those new to computer science, lies in the distinction between data and information. Data refers to raw, unorganized facts. For example, "123," "Smith," and "red" are pieces of data. Information, on the other hand, is processed data that has been given meaning and context. "123 Smith Street" is information derived from the raw data, providing a specific address. The computer system's primary role is to transform data into useful information. This transformation involves organizing, analyzing, and interpreting the raw data to make it meaningful and relevant to the user. As Patterson and Hennessy (2017) explain, "Computer architecture is concerned with how to make the hardware execute the software" (p. 3). This hardware execution, facilitated through the IPOS cycle, is what ultimately transforms data into information. Furthermore, the efficiency and effectiveness of this transformation are key considerations in computer system design, influencing everything from processor architecture to memory organization and storage system performance. Understanding the nuances of the IPOS cycle and the data-information relationship is thus essential for anyone seeking to delve deeper into the world of computer science.

1.3 CAREER PATHS IN COMPUTER SYSTEMS

The field of computer systems presents a diverse landscape of career paths, mirroring the multifaceted nature of the technology itself. Technician roles, often the entry point for many, focus on the practical, hands-on aspects of computer hardware. Technicians are responsible for building, maintaining, and repairing computer systems, troubleshooting hardware issues, and ensuring the smooth operation of computer equipment. Networking professionals design, implement, and manage computer networks, the backbone of modern communication. They ensure seamless data flow between devices, configure network infrastructure (routers, switches, firewalls), and troubleshoot network connectivity problems. Cybersecurity specialists play a crucial role in safeguarding computer systems and networks from an ever-growing array of threats. They protect sensitive data and critical infrastructure from malicious attacks, implementing security protocols, monitoring systems for vulnerabilities, and responding to security incidents. Software engineers, while not strictly focused on "systems" in the hardware sense, are deeply intertwined, developing the software that runs on these systems, from operating systems to application software. Systems administrators manage and maintain computer systems, ensuring their availability, performance, and security. These are just a few examples, and the field is constantly evolving, creating new specializations as technology advances. Cloud computing, artificial intelligence, and data science are just a few areas that are creating a demand for new roles like cloud architects, AI specialists, and data engineers. A frequent question from students contemplating a career in computer systems is, "What skills are most valuable in this field?" While technical expertise is undoubtedly essential, it is no longer sufficient. Soft skills, often overlooked, are equally critical for success. Problem-solving skills are paramount, as computer systems professionals are constantly faced with complex technical challenges. Communication skills are vital for effectively conveying technical information to both technical and non-technical audiences. Teamwork is essential, as most projects involve collaboration with other professionals. Furthermore, the ability to adapt to new technologies is crucial in this rapidly changing field. A commitment to lifelong learning is not just recommended; it's a necessity. As

Stalling and Brown (2018) point out, "The rapid pace of change in computer technology requires professionals to continually update their knowledge and skills" (p. 7). This might involve pursuing certifications, attending conferences, or engaging in self-study. Beyond technical skills and soft skills, a strong understanding of the underlying principles of computer science, such as data structures, algorithms, and operating systems, provides a solid foundation for any career in computer systems. This foundational knowledge allows professionals to adapt to new technologies more easily and to approach problems with a more analytical and systematic mindset. In essence, a successful career in computer systems requires a blend of technical expertise, essential soft skills, a commitment to lifelong learning, and a solid grounding in the fundamentals of computer science.

CHAPTER 2

COMPUTER HARDWARE

FUNDAMENTALS

The bedrock of any computer system resides in its hardware components. These tangible, physical parts work in a coordinated fashion to execute instructions and process data, forming the tangible reality behind the software abstractions. A thorough understanding of their individual functionalities and, perhaps more importantly, their intricate interrelationships is absolutely crucial for anyone working with computer systems, from software developers optimizing code for specific architectures to systems engineers designing complex distributed systems. This knowledge is not merely about knowing the names of components; it's about understanding how they interact, their limitations, and how to leverage their capabilities effectively. For instance, a software developer optimizing a database query needs to understand how data is stored and retrieved from hard drives or SSDs to write efficient queries. Similarly, a systems administrator troubleshooting a network bottleneck needs to understand how network interface cards, switches, and routers work together to transmit data. Consider the scenario of a data center. A cloud provider managing a vast data center needs to consider not only the individual server specifications (CPU, memory, storage) but also how these servers are interconnected, how they are cooled, and how power is distributed. A seemingly simple task like adding more storage to the data center involves a complex understanding of RAID configurations, network storage protocols, and data redundancy techniques. As Hennessy and Patterson (2017) explain, "Computer architecture is the science and art of selecting and interconnecting hardware components to create computers that meet functional, performance,[1] and cost goals" (p. 2). This highlights the importance of understanding the interplay between different hardware components. Furthermore, the evolution of hardware is a continuous process. From the transition from mechanical hard drives to solid-state drives to the rise of specialized hardware like GPUs and FPGAs, computer professionals must stay abreast of these advancements. Understanding the fundamental principles of computer hardware allows them to adapt to these changes and to evaluate the potential impact of new technologies. A common question from students is,

"Why do I need to know about hardware when I'm going to be a software developer?" The answer is that software and hardware are inextricably linked. Software is written to run on specific hardware, and understanding the underlying hardware can significantly impact software performance. For example, understanding cache memory and memory access patterns can help developers write more efficient code. Similarly, understanding the limitations of network bandwidth can help developers design more scalable distributed systems. Therefore, a solid foundation in computer hardware is essential for anyone aspiring to a career in computer science, regardless of their specific area of specialization.

2.1 THE SYSTEM UNIT

The system unit serves as the central repository and protective enclosure for many of a computer system's most vital components. It's far more than a mere metal box; it plays a critical role in safeguarding the delicate internal components from physical damage and, equally importantly, in managing airflow for effective heat dissipation. Consider a modern gaming PC. The system unit houses the motherboard, the central printed circuit board that connects all the components; the CPU, the "brain" of the computer; the RAM modules, providing temporary storage for active processes; the GPU, responsible for graphics processing; storage devices like SSDs or HDDs; and the power supply unit (PSU), providing the necessary electrical power. Without the system unit, these components would be exposed to dust, static electricity, and accidental impacts, significantly increasing the risk of failure. Beyond physical protection, the system unit is crucial for thermal management. Modern CPUs and GPUs generate significant amounts of heat, and without proper cooling, they can overheat and malfunction. The system unit facilitates airflow through strategically placed fans and vents, drawing cool air in and expelling hot air out. This airflow is carefully designed to ensure adequate cooling for all components, preventing thermal throttling and ensuring optimal performance. For high-performance systems, liquid cooling solutions, with their radiators and pumps, are often integrated within the system unit to provide even more efficient heat dissipation. A common question from students is why the design of the system unit matters so much. The answer lies in the intricate relationship between hardware components and their environment. A poorly designed system unit can lead to overheating, component failure, and reduced performance. For example, inadequate airflow can cause the CPU to overheat, leading to reduced clock speeds and slower processing. Similarly, insufficient space within the system unit can make it difficult to install new components or upgrade existing ones. As Clements (2014) notes, "The system unit provides a stable and protected environment for the internal components of a computer system" (p. 87). This stability and protection are essential for ensuring the reliable operation of the computer. Furthermore, the design of the system unit can also impact noise levels. Well-designed system units often incorporate noise-dampening materials and strategically placed fans to minimize noise pollution. In server environments, where numerous servers are housed in close proximity, the system unit's design is even more critical. Effective cooling and efficient airflow management are essential to prevent overheating and ensure the continuous operation of the servers. Therefore, the system unit is not just a container; it's an integral part of the computer system, playing a vital role in protecting components, managing heat, and ensuring optimal performance.

2.1.1 Cases

Computer cases, the enclosures for the core components of a computer system, come in a diverse range of types and form factors, each tailored to specific needs and environments. Tower cases, a common sight in desktop PC setups, offer ample internal space for expansion, accommodating multiple hard drives, high-end graphics cards, and complex cooling solutions. Their larger size allows for better airflow, contributing to cooler operating temperatures and improved component longevity. This makes them a popular choice for gamers, content creators, and enthusiasts who require high performance and future expandability. Smaller form factor (SFF) cases, as the name suggests, prioritize space efficiency. They are designed for environments where space is at a premium, such as home theaters or office workstations. SFF cases come in various sizes, from mini-ITX to micro-ATX, and often require careful component selection to ensure compatibility and adequate cooling within the limited space. Cases also differ significantly in their airflow designs, a crucial factor in system stability and performance. A well-designed case facilitates efficient heat dissipation by creating a consistent airflow path, drawing cool air in and expelling hot air out. This can be achieved through strategically placed fans, vents, and even liquid cooling solutions. Positive pressure systems, where more air is drawn into the case than expelled, can help minimize dust buildup inside the system. Conversely, negative pressure systems, where more air is expelled than drawn in, can be more effective at cooling but may lead to increased dust accumulation. The choice of airflow design depends on the specific needs of the system and the environment in which it will be used. A well-designed case contributes significantly to the longevity and performance of the system. As Muller (2017) emphasizes, "Proper cooling is essential for preventing overheating, which can lead to system instability, component failure, and reduced lifespan" (p. 456). Overheating can cause components to throttle their performance to reduce heat generation, leading to a decrease in overall system performance. In extreme cases, overheating can lead to permanent damage to components, requiring costly repairs or replacements. Consider a professional video editing workstation. Such a system typically includes a powerful CPU, a high-end GPU, and multiple storage drives, all of which generate significant amounts of heat. A poorly designed case with inadequate airflow could lead to overheating, causing the system to crash or the video rendering process to slow down significantly. In contrast, a well-designed case with efficient airflow can prevent these issues, ensuring the system operates reliably and performs optimally. Therefore, selecting the right case is a crucial step in building or upgrading a computer system. It's not just about aesthetics; it's about ensuring the longevity, stability, and performance of the entire system.

2.1.2 Power Supplies

The power supply unit (PSU) is the unsung hero of a computer system, responsible for providing the lifeblood of electricity to all the components. It takes the AC power from the wall outlet and converts it into the various DC voltages required by the motherboard, CPU,

GPU, storage devices, and other peripherals. Choosing the right wattage for a PSU is absolutely crucial; a PSU with insufficient power can lead to a range of problems, from seemingly random system crashes and data corruption to the computer simply failing to boot. Imagine a high-end gaming PC with a powerful GPU and multiple SSDs. These components draw significant power, and if the PSU cannot supply enough wattage, the system may become unstable during demanding games or applications, leading to crashes or even hardware damage. Beyond wattage, PSUs also vary in efficiency, a critical factor to consider in the long run. Efficiency refers to how well the PSU converts AC power to DC power. Higher efficiency ratings, often expressed as a percentage or through certifications like 80 Plus (e.g., 80 Plus Bronze, Silver, Gold, Platinum, Titanium), translate to less wasted energy in the form of heat. This not only reduces electricity bills but also contributes to a cooler and quieter system. Modern PSUs often feature modular designs, a significant improvement over traditional designs. Modular PSUs allow users to connect only the cables they need, reducing cable clutter inside the case and improving airflow. This makes cable management easier and can contribute to better cooling performance. A common misconception, particularly among those new to computer hardware, is that a higher wattage PSU is always better. While having some headroom is advisable, simply buying the highest wattage PSU available is not necessarily the best approach. It's essential to match the PSU's wattage to the system's actual power requirements. Overpowering the system can lead to wasted energy and unnecessary expense. There are online PSU calculators and resources available that can help estimate the power requirements of a specific system configuration. As Horowitz and Hill (2015) explain, "The power supply must be capable of delivering sufficient power to all the components in the system" (p. 672). This involves not only considering the wattage but also the amperage on the various voltage rails (+12V, +5V, +3.3V). Furthermore, the quality of the PSU is just as important as its wattage. A cheap, low-quality PSU can be a fire hazard and may not provide stable power, potentially damaging other components. Therefore, it's crucial to choose a PSU from a reputable manufacturer with a good track record. In a real-world scenario, consider a data center. These facilities house hundreds or even thousands of servers, each requiring a reliable power supply. Efficiency is paramount in this context, as even small improvements in PSU efficiency can translate to significant cost savings and reduced environmental impact. Therefore, selecting the right PSU involves a careful balance of wattage, efficiency, quality, and features like modularity, all tailored to the specific needs of the system.

2.1.3 Motherboards

The motherboard serves as the central nervous system of a computer, acting as the primary hub connecting and coordinating all other components. It's more than just a platform; it dictates fundamental aspects of the system, including the types of CPUs, memory, and expansion cards that can be used, effectively defining the system's capabilities and potential. Motherboards are manufactured in various form factors, such as ATX, Micro-ATX, and Mini-ITX, each designed for different needs and case sizes. ATX, the largest of the common form factors, offers the most expansion slots and connectivity options, making it suitable for high-performance builds. Micro-ATX boards are smaller, offering a balance between size and features, while Mini-ITX boards are the smallest, ideal for space-constrained builds like home theater PCs or small form-factor gaming rigs. The chipset on the motherboard acts as the traffic controller, managing communication between the CPU, memory, and other peripherals. Different chipsets support different features and technologies, influencing factors like memory speed, PCIe lane configurations, and support for integrated graphics. The CPU socket on the motherboard is a crucial element, as it determines the type of processor the motherboard supports. Different CPU manufacturers (like Intel and AMD) use different socket types, and even within the same manufacturer, different generations of CPUs may require different sockets. Expansion slots, such as PCIe slots, provide the interface for installing graphics cards, network cards, sound cards, and other add-on cards, extending the system's functionality. Different PCIe slot versions (e.g., PCIe 3.0, PCIe 4.0) offer varying bandwidth, impacting the performance of high-bandwidth devices like GPUs. Understanding the motherboard's specifications is absolutely critical when building or upgrading a computer system. Choosing the right motherboard ensures compatibility with other components and provides the necessary features and expansion capabilities for the intended use case. For instance, a workstation designed for video editing will likely require a motherboard with multiple PCIe slots for a high-end graphics card and other specialized cards, as well as support for large amounts of RAM. As Silberschatz et al. (2018) discuss, "The motherboard is the central circuit board of a computer, to which all other components are connected" (p. 72). This central role makes motherboard selection a crucial decision. A common question from students is how to choose the right motherboard. The answer depends on several factors, including the intended use of the system, the budget, and the desired features. Researching different motherboard models, reading reviews, and comparing specifications are essential steps in the selection process. Consider a server being built for a database application. Such a server might require a motherboard with support for ECC (Error-Correcting Code) memory for data integrity, multiple network interfaces for high network throughput, and a robust power delivery system to support high-performance processors. Therefore, understanding the intricacies of motherboard specifications and their impact on the overall system is fundamental for anyone working with computer hardware.

2.2 CORE COMPONENTS

These components are essential for the computer's basic functionality.

2.2.1 Processors (CPU)

The Central Processing Unit (CPU), often dubbed the "brain" of the computer, is the linchpin of computation, responsible for executing instructions and performing the myriad calculations that underpin all software operations. Its performance is a complex equation, influenced by several key factors. Clock speed, traditionally measured in GHz, indicates the frequency at which the CPU executes instructions. While a higher clock speed generally suggests faster processing, it's not the sole determinant of performance. The number of cores within the CPU significantly impacts its ability to handle multiple tasks concurrently. Modern CPUs often boast multiple cores, enabling parallel processing and dramatically improving performance, especially in multi-threaded applications. Imagine a video editing software rendering a complex scene; a multi-core CPU can divide the rendering task among its cores, completing the process much faster than a single-core CPU. Cache size, a small, high-speed memory within the CPU, stores frequently accessed data and instructions. By reducing the need to access slower main memory, cache significantly improves processing efficiency. Different levels of cache (L1, L2, L3) exist, each with varying sizes and speeds, forming a hierarchical memory system within the CPU. The architecture of the CPU, such as x86 (predominant in desktop and laptop computers) or ARM (commonly found in mobile devices), plays a crucial role in its performance and, critically, its compatibility with software. Software is often compiled for specific architectures, meaning that software designed for an x86 processor will not run natively on an ARM processor without emulation, which can introduce performance overhead. As Hennessy and Patterson (2017) explain, "Computer architecture is concerned with the design of the CPU, the memory system, and the I/O system" (p. 3). The CPU, as the heart of the system, is a central focus of computer architecture. A common question arises regarding the choice between CPUs with higher clock speeds versus those with more cores. The optimal choice depends on the intended workload. Applications that are heavily multi-threaded, like video editing software or 3D rendering programs, benefit significantly from multiple cores. However, some applications, especially older ones, may not be optimized for multi-threading and may see more benefit from a higher clock speed. Consider a database server handling numerous concurrent requests. In this scenario, a CPU with many cores would be more advantageous, as each core can handle a separate request, improving overall throughput. Conversely, a single-threaded application, such as an older game, might perform better on a CPU with a higher clock speed. Therefore, understanding the interplay between clock speed, core count, cache size, and architecture is essential for selecting the right CPU for a specific application. Furthermore, advancements in CPU technology, such as new instruction sets and manufacturing processes, continually impact CPU performance and efficiency, requiring computer professionals to stay abreast of these developments.

2.2.2 Memory (RAM)

Random Access Memory (RAM) serves as the computer's primary working memory, a crucial component holding the data and instructions that the CPU is actively using. Think of it as the CPU's short-term memory, allowing for rapid access to the information needed for immediate processing. A key characteristic of RAM is its volatility; its contents are lost when the computer is powered off. This is why we have persistent storage devices like hard drives and SSDs to save data for long-term use. Different types of RAM exist, with DDR4 and DDR5 being prominent examples. Newer generations, like DDR5, offer faster speeds and improved performance compared to their predecessors, allowing the CPU to access data more quickly. The amount of RAM available in a system is a critical factor in overall performance, particularly when running memory-intensive applications. Consider a video editing workflow. Large video files, often gigabytes in size, need to be loaded into RAM for editing. Insufficient RAM would force the system to constantly swap data between RAM and the much slower storage drive, a process known as "paging," leading to significant performance bottlenecks and a frustratingly slow editing experience. Similarly, running multiple applications simultaneously, such as a web browser with numerous tabs, a word processor, and a graphics editor, demands sufficient RAM to prevent slowdowns and ensure smooth multitasking. As Patterson and Hennessy (2017) explain, "Memory hierarchy is a fundamental concept in computer organization, designed to provide fast access to frequently used data" (p. 345). RAM sits at the top of this hierarchy, providing the fastest but most volatile access. A common question students ask is how much RAM is "enough." The answer is context-dependent and tied to the user's typical workload. For basic tasks like web browsing and email, 8GB of RAM might suffice. However, for more demanding tasks like gaming, video editing, 3D modeling, or running virtual machines, 16GB, 32GB, or even more RAM might be necessary. Consider a scientific simulation running on a high-performance computing cluster. These simulations often involve massive datasets and complex calculations, requiring vast amounts of RAM to store the data and intermediate results. Insufficient RAM could limit the size and complexity of the simulations that can be run. Therefore, understanding the role of RAM, its different types, and its impact on performance is essential for anyone working with computer systems, whether it's a software developer optimizing memory usage in their code or a system administrator configuring servers for optimal performance. Choosing the right amount and type of RAM is a crucial decision in building a computer system that meets the user's needs and budget.

2.3 STORAGE DEVICES

These devices store data persistently, even when the computer is powered off.

2.3.1 Hard Disk Drives (HDD)

Hard Disk Drives (HDDs) have long been a staple in computer systems, providing mass storage for data and applications. They function by storing data magnetically on spinning platters, much like a record player stores audio. This mechanical nature is both their strength and their weakness. HDDs offer large storage capacities at a relatively low cost per gigabyte, making them a cost-effective solution for storing vast amounts of data, such as large media libraries, backups, or archives. However, their mechanical nature also makes them significantly slower than Solid State Drives (SSDs), which have no moving parts. The speed at which an HDD can read and write data is limited by the rotational speed of the platters and the speed of the read/write head that accesses the data. Imagine trying to quickly find a specific song on a vinyl record compared to instantly accessing it on a digital music player; this analogy illustrates the speed difference

31

between HDDs and SSDs. The interface used to connect the HDD to the motherboard also plays a role in its performance. SATA (Serial ATA) is the most common interface for HDDs, offering reasonable data transfer speeds. However, newer interfaces like NVMe (Non-Volatile Memory Express), primarily used for SSDs, offer significantly higher bandwidth and are not typically used for traditional HDDs due to their mechanical limitations. While some enterprise-grade HDDs might use SAS (Serial Attached SCSI) for higher performance, SATA remains the dominant interface for consumer-grade HDDs. A common question from students is why HDDs are still used given their slower speeds compared to SSDs. The primary reason is cost. HDDs offer a much lower cost per gigabyte than SSDs, making them a more economical choice for storing large amounts of data where access speed is not the primary concern. Consider a large data center storing archival data. Petabytes of data need to be stored, and the cost of using SSDs for all that data would be prohibitive. HDDs, in this scenario, offer a practical and cost-effective solution. As Stallings (2018) explains, "Secondary storage is used to hold data and programs that are not currently in use by the CPU" (p. 225). HDDs serve this purpose admirably, providing persistent storage for large amounts of data. Another real-world example is a Network Attached Storage (NAS) device used for home or small business backups. These devices often utilize multiple HDDs in RAID configurations to provide redundancy and large storage capacity at a reasonable price. Therefore, while SSDs have become the preferred choice for primary storage due to their speed, HDDs continue to play a vital role in scenarios where cost and capacity are more important than raw speed. They remain a relevant and practical technology for specific use cases, especially in the realm of mass storage and archiving.

2.3.2 Solid State Drives (SSD)

Solid State Drives (SSDs) have revolutionized data storage, offering a paradigm shift in speed and performance compared to traditional Hard Disk Drives (HDDs). SSDs store data in flash memory chips, similar to the technology used in USB drives, but on a much larger and more sophisticated scale. This lack of moving parts is the key to their superior performance. Because SSDs don't rely on spinning platters and read/write heads, they offer significantly faster read and write speeds, resulting in quicker boot times, faster application loading, and a dramatically improved overall system responsiveness.

Imagine a computer booting up in seconds rather than minutes, or applications launching instantaneously; this is the kind of performance boost SSDs provide. SSDs come in various form factors, including SATA, NVMe, and M.2. SATA SSDs, while still faster than HDDs, utilize the same interface as traditional hard drives, limiting their performance potential. NVMe (Non-Volatile Memory Express) drives, on the other hand, are designed specifically for high-performance storage and utilize the PCIe bus, offering significantly higher bandwidth and thus much faster speeds. M.2 is a form factor that can house both SATA and NVMe SSDs; an M.2 SSD using the NVMe protocol will deliver the highest performance. As Silberschatz et al. (2018) explain, "Solid-state drives (SSDs) are nonvolatile storage devices that use flash memory to store data" (p. 287). This non-volatility, combined with their speed, makes them ideal for primary storage, where operating systems and frequently used applications reside. A common question is why someone would still use an HDD when SSDs are so much faster. The primary reason, as discussed previously, is cost. SSDs typically have a higher cost per gigabyte compared to HDDs. Therefore, while SSDs are excellent for primary storage, HDDs remain a viable option for secondary storage, archiving, or storing large amounts of data where access speed is not the top priority. Consider a professional video editor working with large 4K video files. An NVMe SSD would be ideal for storing the actively edited project files, allowing for smooth playback and fast rendering. However, the editor might use a large HDD to store archived video footage or completed projects, where access speed is less critical. Another real-world example is cloud computing. Cloud providers often use a tiered storage system, with SSDs for high-performance applications and HDDs for less demanding workloads, optimizing both performance and cost. Therefore, understanding the different types of SSDs, their performance characteristics, and their cost implications is crucial for making informed decisions about storage solutions. The choice between SSDs and HDDs, or a combination of both, depends on the specific needs and budget of the user or organization.

2.3.3 Optical Drives

Optical drives, once a ubiquitous component in computer systems, read and write data to optical discs such as CDs, DVDs, and Blu-ray discs. These drives utilize lasers to read data from the disc's surface and, in the case of writable drives, to burn data onto the disc. While their prevalence has diminished significantly with the rise of USB drives, cloud storage, and readily available high-speed internet access, optical drives still retain niche applications. They can be used for installing software, particularly older software that may not be readily available for download, or for playing media such as movies or music stored on optical discs. Consider a scenario where a user needs to install specialized software that is only distributed on a DVD. An optical drive would be necessary to access and install this software. Similarly, individuals with large collections of movies or music on Blu-ray discs might still use optical drives for playback. Although less common in modern desktop computers and laptops, optical drives are sometimes found in specialized systems, such as industrial control systems or embedded systems, where backwards compatibility with older media formats might be required. As Stallings (2018) notes, "Optical storage devices use lasers to read and write data" (p. 245).

This laser technology allows for relatively high storage densities, especially with Blu-ray discs, which can hold significantly more data than DVDs or CDs. A common question is why optical drives are becoming less common. The primary reason is the convenience and accessibility of other storage and distribution methods. USB drives offer portability and ease of use, while cloud storage provides access to data from anywhere with an internet connection. Digital distribution of software and media has also become the dominant method, making physical media like optical discs less necessary. However, it's important to recognize that optical drives still serve a purpose in certain situations. For instance, in regions with limited internet access, physical media might still be a more reliable way to distribute software or media. Similarly, for archiving purposes, optical discs, especially M-DISCs, which are designed for long-term data preservation, might still be considered a viable option. Therefore, while optical drives are not as essential as they once were, they haven't completely disappeared. They continue to be relevant for specific use cases, particularly those involving legacy software, media playback, or situations where alternative storage and distribution methods are not readily available or practical.

2.3.4 Removable Storage

Removable storage solutions, such as USB drives and SD cards, offer convenient and portable ways to transfer and store data between devices. These small, yet powerful, storage devices have become ubiquitous in modern computing, serving a multitude of purposes from simple file transfers to backing up critical data. USB drives, also known as flash drives or thumb drives, connect to computers via the USB port, a standard interface found on virtually all modern computers. They utilize flash memory to store data, making them durable and resistant to physical damage compared to older removable storage solutions like floppy disks. SD (Secure Digital) cards, on the other hand, are commonly used in digital cameras, smartphones, and other portable devices. They also employ flash memory technology and come in various sizes and capacities, offering flexibility for different storage needs. Both USB drives and SD cards are widely used for storing documents, photos, videos, and other files, facilitating easy sharing and transportation of data. Imagine a student working on a project at school. They can save their work on a USB drive and then easily transfer it to their home computer to continue working. Similarly, a photographer can use SD cards to store the photos taken with their digital camera, and then transfer those photos to their computer for editing and sharing. As Tanenbaum and Bos (2015) explain, "Removable storage devices allow users to easily transport data between computers" (p. 312). This portability is a key advantage, enabling users to work on files across different devices without needing a network connection. A common question is what the difference is between USB drives and SD cards. While both use flash memory, they differ in form factor and typical applications. USB drives are generally larger and connect directly to a USB port, making them convenient for transferring files between computers. SD cards, being smaller, are often used in devices with limited space, such as cameras and mobile phones. They often require an adapter to connect to a standard USB port on a computer. Consider a professional videographer. They might use multiple SD cards to record footage during a shoot and then use a card reader connected to their laptop to transfer the footage for editing. They might also use a ruggedized external hard drive, connected via USB, for on-site backups of the captured video files. Therefore, understanding the characteristics and applications of removable storage devices is essential in today's digital world. From simple file transfers to data backups and media storage,

USB drives and SD cards play a crucial role in our personal and professional lives. Choosing the right type and capacity of removable storage depends on the specific needs of the user and the devices they are using.

2.4 INPUT/OUTPUT DEVICES

These devices allow users to interact with the computer system.

2.4.1 Input Devices

Input devices form the crucial bridge between human users and the digital world of computers, enabling the entry of data and commands that drive all computational processes. Keyboards, the most traditional input device, allow for textual input, enabling users to type documents, write code, and interact with software applications. Mice, along with touchpads, provide a pointing interface, allowing for precise cursor control and interaction with graphical user interfaces. These devices are essential for navigating operating systems, manipulating files, and interacting with applications in a visually intuitive manner. Scanners digitize physical documents and images, converting them into digital formats that can be stored, edited, and shared on a computer. This is invaluable in fields like archiving, document management, and graphic design. Webcams capture video and still images, enabling video conferencing, live streaming, and other visual communication. They are essential tools for remote collaboration, social media, and security surveillance. Beyond these common examples, input devices also encompass a wide range of specialized tools. Microphones capture audio input, enabling voice commands, dictation, and recording of music or sound effects. Touchscreens, increasingly prevalent on mobile devices and some laptops, allow for direct interaction with the display using fingers or styluses. Game controllers, such as joysticks and gamepads, provide specialized input for gaming, allowing for complex character movement and interaction within virtual worlds. Biometric scanners, like fingerprint readers, enhance security by verifying user identity. As Tanenbaum and Bos (2015) explain, "Input devices allow humans to communicate with the computer" (p. 295). This communication is fundamental to all computer usage, from simple tasks like writing an email to complex operations like designing a building using CAD software. A common question students ask is how to choose the right input device. The answer depends heavily on the specific task and user preferences. For example, a graphic designer might prefer a drawing tablet with a stylus for precise control, while a programmer might prioritize a mechanical keyboard with tactile feedback for comfortable typing. Consider a musician using a digital audio workstation (DAW).

They might use a MIDI keyboard as an input device to create music, recording notes and controlling virtual instruments within the software. They might also use a microphone to record vocals or acoustic instruments. Therefore, understanding the diverse range of input devices available and their specific functionalities is essential for anyone working with computers. Choosing the right input device can significantly enhance productivity, efficiency, and user experience. Furthermore, the development of new and innovative input devices continues to expand the ways in which humans interact with computers, opening up new possibilities in fields like virtual reality, augmented reality, and human-computer interaction.

2.4.2 Output Devices

Output devices serve as the crucial link in translating the results of computer processing into a human-understandable format, presenting information to the user. Monitors, the most common output device, visually display information, ranging from simple text documents to complex graphical interfaces and high-definition videos. They come in various types, including LCD (Liquid Crystal Display), LED (Light Emitting Diode), and OLED (Organic Light Emitting Diode), each with its own characteristics in terms of image quality, power consumption, and cost. Resolution, measured in pixels, dictates the sharpness and detail of the displayed image. Higher resolutions result in more detailed and crisp images, crucial for tasks like graphic design, video editing, and gaming. Printers produce hard copies of digital documents and images. They also vary significantly in type, with inkjet printers being popular for home use due to their lower initial cost and ability to print color images. Laser printers, on the other hand, are often preferred in office environments for their faster printing speeds and ability to handle large print volumes. Beyond these common output devices, speakers translate digital audio signals into sound, enabling users to listen to music, watch videos with sound, and participate in voice communication. Specialized output devices also exist, catering to specific needs. Projectors display images onto large surfaces, ideal for presentations and large-screen viewing experiences. 3D printers create physical objects from digital designs, revolutionizing fields like prototyping, manufacturing, and even medicine. As Tanenbaum and Bos (2015) explain, "Output devices allow the computer to communicate with the outside world" (p. 305). This communication is essential for users to interact with and benefit from the processing power of computers. A common question is how to choose the right output device. The answer depends on the specific application and user requirements. For example, a graphic designer might prioritize a high-resolution monitor with accurate color reproduction, while a business user might need a fast and reliable laser printer. Consider a scenario in a medical imaging department. Radiologists require high-resolution monitors with specialized features to accurately view and interpret medical images, such as X-rays and CT scans. The accuracy and clarity of these images are critical for diagnosis and treatment planning. Therefore, understanding the diverse range of output devices available and their specific functionalities is crucial for both users and computer professionals. Choosing the right output device can significantly impact productivity, efficiency, and the overall user experience. Furthermore, the continued development of new output technologies, such as virtual reality headsets and holographic displays, promises to further expand the ways in which humans interact with and experience digital information.

2.5 PERIPHERAL DEVICES AND INTERFACES

These devices extend the functionality of the computer system.

2.5.1 Adapter Cards

Adapter cards, also known as expansion cards, extend the functionality of a computer system by providing specialized capabilities beyond the core features offered by the motherboard. These cards plug into expansion slots on the motherboard, such as PCIe slots, and offer a range of functionalities, from enhanced graphics processing to network connectivity and high-fidelity audio. Graphics cards, perhaps the most well-known type of adapter card, significantly enhance video output and gaming performance. They feature dedicated GPUs (Graphics Processing Units) that offload graphics processing from the CPU, resulting in smoother frame rates, higher resolutions, and improved visual fidelity in games and other graphics-intensive applications. Consider a professional video editor working with high-resolution footage. A powerful graphics card is essential for smooth playback, real-time editing, and fast rendering of video effects. Similarly, gamers rely on graphics cards to achieve immersive gaming experiences with high frame rates and detailed graphics. Network cards enable a computer to connect to a network, whether it's a wired Ethernet connection or a wireless Wi-Fi connection. These cards handle the communication protocols and physical interface required for network connectivity, allowing computers to access the internet, share files, and communicate with other devices on the network. A common scenario is a business network where employees need to access shared files and applications on a server. Network cards in each workstation facilitate this connectivity. Sound cards provide high-quality audio output, offering superior sound fidelity compared to the integrated audio on most motherboards. They often feature dedicated audio processors and higher-quality audio components, resulting in richer and more immersive audio experiences. While integrated audio has improved significantly, audiophiles and professionals working with audio often prefer dedicated sound cards for their superior audio quality. As Stallings (2018) explains, "Expansion cards provide additional functionality to the computer system" (p. 267). This added functionality allows users to customize their systems to meet their specific needs. A common question is why someone would need a separate adapter card when similar functionality is already integrated into the motherboard. The answer often comes down to performance, features, or specialized requirements. For example, while most motherboards have integrated graphics, a dedicated graphics card offers significantly higher performance for gaming or graphics-intensive tasks. Similarly, a professional musician might need a sound card with specific inputs and outputs for their audio equipment. Consider a scientific research lab using a high-performance computing cluster. These clusters often utilize specialized network cards, such as InfiniBand adapters, to provide very high bandwidth and low latency communication between the nodes in the cluster, essential for running complex simulations. Therefore, understanding the different types of adapter cards available and their specific functionalities is crucial for building or upgrading a computer system. Choosing the right adapter cards can significantly enhance the performance, capabilities, and overall user experience of a computer.

2.5.2 Ports and Cables

Ports and cables form the essential physical connections between a computer and its peripheral devices, enabling the flow of data and power that brings the system to life. These connections are not merely passive conduits; the type of port and cable used significantly impacts the speed, reliability, and even the type of data that can be transmitted. USB (Universal Serial Bus) ports are ubiquitous, serving as a versatile interface for a wide range of devices, from mice and keyboards to external hard drives and printers. Different USB versions (e.g., USB 2.0, USB 3.0, USB-C) offer varying data transfer speeds, with newer versions providing significantly faster data transfer, crucial for devices like external SSDs or high-resolution webcams. HDMI (High-Definition Multimedia Interface) ports and cables are the standard for connecting displays, transmitting both video and audio signals digitally. Different HDMI versions support different resolutions and refresh rates, making it essential to choose the right cable for high-definition displays and gaming monitors. DisplayPort offers similar functionality to HDMI, often preferred for connecting multiple monitors or high-end graphics cards. Ethernet ports and cables provide wired network connectivity, offering reliable and high-speed internet access. Different Ethernet cable categories (e.g., Cat5e, Cat6, Cat6a) support different speeds, with newer categories capable of handling gigabit and even multi-gigabit network connections, essential for data centers and high-bandwidth applications. Audio jacks provide connections for headphones and microphones, enabling audio input and output. Different types of audio jacks exist, such as 3.5mm and 6.35mm, each commonly used for different audio equipment. As Stallings (2018) points out, "The I/O modules provide a means of exchanging data between the computer and the outside world" (p. 289). Ports and cables are the physical manifestation of these I/O modules. A common question from students is how to choose the right cable for a specific connection. The answer depends on the type of device being connected, the type of data being transmitted, and the desired performance. For instance, connecting a 4K monitor requires an HDMI cable that supports the necessary bandwidth for that resolution. Similarly, connecting to a gigabit network requires an Ethernet cable of at least Cat5e or higher category. Consider a professional audio engineer setting up a recording studio. They might use a combination of USB ports for connecting MIDI keyboards and audio interfaces, XLR cables for connecting microphones, and TRS cables for connecting studio monitors. Understanding the different types of ports and cables, their functionalities, and their limitations is crucial for anyone working with computer systems. Using the correct cable ensures optimal performance, prevents compatibility issues, and avoids potential damage to devices. Furthermore, staying informed about the latest advancements in port and cable technology, such as Thunderbolt and USB4, is essential for keeping up with the evolving landscape of computer connectivity.

2.6 COOLING SYSTEMS

Cooling is essential to prevent overheating and ensure the stability and longevity of computer components.

2.6.1 Fans

Fans are essential components within a computer system, playing a crucial role in thermal management by circulating air within the system unit. Their primary function is to dissipate the heat generated by components like the CPU and GPU, preventing overheating and ensuring stable system operation. Without adequate cooling, these components can reach temperatures that lead to performance throttling, system instability, and even permanent damage. Fans come in various sizes and types, each designed for specific airflow and noise characteristics. Larger fans generally move more air at lower RPMs, often resulting in quieter operation. Smaller fans, while potentially more compact, typically need to spin at higher speeds to achieve similar airflow, which can lead to increased noise levels. Different fan types also exist, including axial fans, which move air parallel to their axis of rotation, and centrifugal fans, which move air perpendicular to their axis. Axial fans are more common in computer systems due to their efficiency and compact size. As Horowitz and Hill (2015) explain, "Cooling is essential for reliable operation of electronic equipment" (p. 702). This is particularly true for high-performance CPUs and GPUs, which can generate significant amounts of heat. A common question is how to choose the right fans for a computer system. The answer depends on several factors, including the amount of heat generated by the components, the size of the system unit, and the desired noise level. Consider a gaming PC with a high-end GPU. Such a system requires robust cooling to maintain optimal performance during demanding games. In this case, high-performance fans with good airflow and potentially a liquid cooling solution might be necessary. On the other hand, a home theater PC, where quiet operation is a priority, might benefit from larger, slower-spinning fans or fans with noise-dampening features. Another real-world example is a data center, where hundreds or thousands of servers are housed in close proximity. Effective cooling is absolutely critical in data centers to prevent overheating and ensure the continuous operation of the servers. Data centers often employ sophisticated cooling systems, including large fans, liquid cooling, and even air conditioning, to maintain optimal temperatures. Therefore, understanding the different types of fans, their airflow characteristics, and their noise levels is crucial for building and maintaining computer systems. Choosing the right fans ensures that the system operates reliably and efficiently, preventing overheating and prolonging the lifespan of the components. Furthermore, the design and implementation of effective cooling solutions are essential considerations in various computing environments, from individual PCs to large-scale data centers.

2.6.2 Heatsinks

Heatsinks are integral components in thermal management within computer systems, acting as passive heat exchangers that draw heat away from components like the CPU and GPU. They are designed to increase the surface area available for heat dissipation, effectively transferring heat from the component to the surrounding air. Heatsinks are typically made of thermally conductive materials, such as aluminum or copper, and feature a series of fins or other structures that maximize their surface area. They are often attached to the component using thermal paste or thermal pads, which improve the thermal contact between the heatsink and the component, facilitating more efficient heat transfer. Heatsinks are frequently used in conjunction with fans to provide a more effective cooling solution. The fan forces air across the heatsink's fins, further enhancing heat dissipation and preventing the component from overheating. As Bar-Cohen and Kraus (2015) explain, "Heat sinks are passive thermal devices that transfer heat from a hot component to a cooler fluid" (p. 123). This passive heat transfer is crucial for maintaining the operating temperatures of sensitive electronic components within safe limits. A common question is why heatsinks are necessary. The answer lies in the fact that electronic components, particularly CPUs and GPUs, generate significant amounts of heat during operation. Without proper cooling, these components can reach temperatures that lead to performance throttling, system instability, and even permanent damage. Heatsinks provide a passive means of dissipating this heat, preventing these issues and ensuring the reliable operation of the system. Consider a high-performance gaming laptop. These laptops pack powerful CPUs and GPUs into a relatively small form factor, generating a considerable amount of heat. Heatsinks, often combined with fans and vapor chambers, are essential for keeping these components cool and preventing thermal throttling, which would reduce gaming performance. Another real-world example is in server farms, where numerous servers are housed in close proximity. Effective cooling is paramount in these environments to prevent overheating and ensure the continuous operation of the servers. Heatsinks, often used in conjunction with liquid cooling solutions, play a crucial role in maintaining the operating temperatures of the server CPUs and preventing downtime. Therefore, understanding the principles of heat transfer and the role of heatsinks in thermal management is essential for anyone working with computer hardware. Choosing the right heatsink for a specific component depends on factors like the amount of heat generated by the component, the available space within the system, and the desired noise level. Furthermore, the design and implementation of effective cooling solutions are critical considerations in a wide range of computing environments, from individual PCs to large-scale data centers.

2.6.3 Liquid Cooling

Liquid cooling systems represent a significant advancement in thermal management for computer systems, employing a liquid coolant to efficiently transfer heat away from critical components. Unlike traditional air cooling, which relies on the circulation of air to dissipate heat, liquid cooling utilizes a closed-loop system where a liquid coolant absorbs heat from the components and then transfers that heat to a radiator, where it is dissipated into the surrounding air. This process allows for significantly more efficient heat transfer compared to air cooling, making liquid cooling a popular choice for high-performance systems that generate substantial amounts of heat. These systems typically consist of a water block, which is attached to the component (CPU or GPU) and absorbs the heat; tubing, which carries the heated coolant away from the water block; a radiator, which dissipates the heat from the coolant; and a pump, which circulates the coolant through the system. Some systems also include a reservoir to hold extra coolant and help manage air bubbles in the system. As Bar-Cohen and Kraus (2015) explain, "Liquid cooling offers higher heat transfer coefficients than air cooling" (p. 257). This translates to more effective heat dissipation and the ability to cool components that generate significantly more heat than air cooling can handle. A common question is why liquid cooling is preferred in some systems. The answer lies in its superior cooling performance. High-performance CPUs and GPUs, especially when overclocked, can generate immense amounts of heat. Air cooling, even with high-end heatsinks and fans, may not be sufficient to keep these components within their safe operating temperatures. Liquid cooling provides the necessary cooling capacity to prevent thermal throttling and ensure stable system operation under heavy load. Consider a high-performance workstation used for 3D rendering or video editing. These tasks place a significant load on the CPU and GPU, generating a lot of heat. A liquid cooling system would be essential in this scenario to prevent overheating and maintain optimal performance. Another real-world example is in data centers, where numerous servers are packed into a small space. Effective cooling is absolutely critical in these environments, and liquid cooling is often employed to manage the heat generated by the servers and maintain a stable operating environment. Furthermore, liquid cooling systems can often operate more quietly than high-performance air cooling solutions. While the pump in a liquid cooling system does produce some noise, it is often less than the noise generated by multiple high-speed fans needed for comparable air cooling performance. Therefore, understanding the principles of liquid cooling and its advantages over air cooling is important for anyone working with high-performance computer systems. Choosing the right liquid cooling system depends on factors like the amount of heat generated by the components, the available space within the system, and the desired noise level. Liquid cooling has become increasingly accessible and is now a common solution not just for servers and workstations but also for enthusiast-built PCs where performance is paramount.

CHAPTER 3

PC ASSEMBLY AND

DISASSEMBLY

The ability to assemble and disassemble a personal computer is a foundational skill for any aspiring computer technician, IT professional, or even a dedicated enthusiast. It provides invaluable hands-on experience with the intricate hardware components that make up a computer system, fostering a deeper understanding of how these components interact and function as a cohesive unit. This practical knowledge is not merely about following instructions; it's about developing a mental model of the system, enabling effective troubleshooting, upgrades, and repairs. This section will delve into the essential procedures involved in PC assembly and disassembly, emphasizing crucial safety precautions to prevent damage to components or injury to the individual, and outlining the necessary tools for a successful and efficient process. Consider a scenario where a system administrator needs to upgrade the RAM in a server. Understanding the proper disassembly procedures to access the memory slots, the correct way to handle the delicate RAM modules, and the reassembly process to ensure proper seating and connectivity is crucial. Similarly, a computer technician troubleshooting a faulty PC needs to be able to systematically disassemble the system to isolate the problem component, whether it's a failing power supply or a malfunctioning hard drive. As Mueller (2017) details in his comprehensive PC hardware book, "Understanding the installation and configuration of PC components is essential for anyone working with computers" (p. 125). This underscores the importance of practical, hands-on skills in the field. A common question from those new to PC building is where to begin. The process starts with careful planning, including selecting compatible components (CPU, motherboard, RAM, storage, etc.) based on the intended use of the system. Then comes the physical assembly, starting with installing the CPU on the motherboard, followed by RAM modules, and then mounting the motherboard in the case. Connecting the various cables (power supply, data cables, front panel connectors) requires attention to detail and a clear understanding of each component's function. Disassembly, while seemingly the reverse of assembly, also requires careful attention to avoid damaging components. Static electricity is a major concern, and using an anti-static wrist strap is crucial. Proper handling of components, especially delicate ones like the CPU and RAM, is essential. A real-world example highlighting the importance of these skills is in a small business setting. A small business owner might rely on a local computer technician to build and maintain their office computers. The technician's ability to assemble reliable systems, diagnose hardware issues, and perform necessary repairs quickly and efficiently is crucial for the smooth operation of the business. Therefore, mastering PC assembly and disassembly is not just a technical skill; it's a valuable asset in a wide range of situations, from troubleshooting a personal computer to maintaining complex server systems.

3.1 SAFETY PRECAUTIONS (ESD PROTECTION)

Electrostatic discharge (ESD) poses a significant threat to the delicate electronic components within a computer system. Even a seemingly minor static shock from the human body can irreparably damage sensitive parts like the CPU, RAM modules, or the motherboard itself. Therefore, taking proper ESD precautions is not just recommended; it's absolutely paramount during any PC assembly or disassembly procedure. The most common and effective method for mitigating ESD risk is using an anti-static wrist strap. This strap, worn around the wrist, is connected to a grounded point, such as the metal chassis of the computer case, providing a continuous path for any static charge to dissipate safely. This grounding prevents the buildup of static electricity on the body, effectively neutralizing the threat to sensitive components. Working on a static-free surface, such as an anti-static mat, further enhances ESD protection. These mats are designed to dissipate static electricity and provide a safe working environment for handling electronic components. Avoid working on carpets, as they are notorious for generating static electricity. Similarly, wearing clothing made of synthetic materials, which are prone to static buildup, should be avoided if possible. When handling components, it's crucial to always hold them by their edges, avoiding direct contact with the pins, circuitry, or any exposed electronic parts. This simple practice minimizes the risk of ESD damage. A common misconception, particularly among those new to PC building, is that briefly touching a grounded metal object before handling components is sufficient. While this action can help discharge some static electricity, it's not a reliable long-term solution. The charge can quickly build up again, and there's no guarantee of complete discharge. An anti-static wrist strap, on the other hand, provides continuous grounding, offering much more robust protection. As Mueller (2017) emphasizes, "ESD damage is a real threat, and proper precautions must be taken to prevent it" (p. 187). This underscores the importance of adhering to established ESD safety protocols. Consider a scenario where a technician is upgrading the memory in a server. Without proper ESD protection, they risk damaging the new RAM modules during installation, rendering them unusable. This could lead to downtime for the server, impacting business operations. Therefore, understanding the risks of ESD and implementing the recommended precautions is crucial for anyone working with computer hardware. It's not just about protecting the components; it's about ensuring the reliability and longevity of the entire system. Taking the time to use an anti-static wrist strap and following other ESD safety practices is a small investment that can save time, money, and frustration in the long run.

3.2 TOOLS AND EQUIPMENT

Equipping oneself with the appropriate tools is absolutely essential for efficient and safe PC assembly and disassembly. Attempting to work on delicate electronic components with improper tools can lead to frustration, damage to hardware, and even personal injury. A well-stocked basic toolkit should include a set of Phillips head screwdrivers in various sizes to accommodate the different screws used in PC construction. A flat-head screwdriver can be useful for certain tasks, such as prying open stubborn latches or connectors. Pliers can be helpful for manipulating small components or cables, while tweezers are invaluable for handling tiny screws or connectors in tight spaces. Cable ties are essential for organized cable management, improving airflow within the system unit and making future upgrades or repairs easier. A magnetic parts tray is a small but incredibly useful tool for keeping screws, standoffs, and other small components organized during the assembly process, preventing them from getting lost or rolling away. As previously emphasized, an anti-static wrist strap and an anti-static mat are non-negotiable for ESD protection. A flashlight or headlamp can be surprisingly useful when working inside the dimly lit confines of a computer case, allowing for clear visibility of components and connections. For more advanced troubleshooting and diagnostics, a multimeter is an invaluable tool. It allows technicians to test power supply voltages, check for continuity in circuits, and diagnose a range of electrical problems. As Mueller (2017) explains, "Having the proper tools not only makes the job easier, but also helps to prevent damage to the components" (p. 201). This highlights the importance of investing in quality tools. A common question that arises is whether specialized tools are always necessary. While a basic toolkit will suffice for most common assembly and disassembly tasks, certain specialized tools may be required for specific situations. For example, when reapplying thermal paste to a CPU cooler, a heat gun or specialized thermal paste applicator might be beneficial. Similarly, creating custom cables or repairing damaged cables might require a crimping tool and other specialized connectors. Consider a network technician installing new network cables in a server room. They might need a cable tester to verify the connections and a crimping tool to terminate the cables with RJ-45 connectors. Another example is a system builder working with custom liquid cooling solutions. They might need specialized tools for bending tubing, installing fittings, and leak testing the system. Therefore, while a basic toolkit is a great starting point, it's important to recognize when specialized tools are necessary and to invest in them as needed. Having the right tool for the job not only makes the task easier and more efficient but also helps to prevent damage to components and ensures a professional and reliable outcome.

3.3 STEP-BY-STEP PC ASSEMBLY (FROM CASE TO BOOT-UP)

Assembling a PC is a systematic and methodical process that requires careful attention to detail to avoid errors and ensure a functional system. The process begins with installing the CPU onto the motherboard, a delicate operation that requires ensuring the CPU is correctly aligned with the socket and gently seated. Applying thermal paste or using a pre-applied thermal solution on the CPU cooler is essential for effective heat transfer. Next, the RAM modules are installed into their designated slots on the motherboard, making sure they are fully seated and the retaining clips are engaged. The motherboard is then carefully mounted into the case, securing it with standoffs and screws. Storage devices, whether HDDs or SSDs, are installed in their respective bays, ensuring they are properly secured. Connecting the necessary cables from the power supply to the motherboard, storage devices, and other components is a critical step. This includes the main 24-pin ATX power connector, the 8-pin EPS connector for the CPU, and SATA power connectors for the storage

69

drives. Any expansion cards, such as a graphics card, are then installed into their appropriate slots on the motherboard, usually PCIe slots. Finally, the front panel connectors, including the power button, reset button, USB ports, and audio jacks, are connected to the motherboard's front panel header, following the motherboard manual's instructions. Once all the components are connected, it's crucial to double-check all connections, ensuring they are firmly seated. Then, the system can be powered on. The system should perform a POST (Power On Self-Test), a series of diagnostic checks that verify the functionality of the hardware. If all goes well, the system will proceed to boot, ideally leading to the operating system installation process. A frequent challenge faced by beginners, and even experienced builders, is cable management. Proper cable management is not merely about aesthetics; it significantly improves airflow within the case, contributing to better cooling performance and preventing components from overheating. It also makes troubleshooting and future upgrades much easier, as cables are neatly organized and accessible. As Mueller (2017) explains, "Proper cable management is essential for good airflow and easy access to components" (p. 235). This highlights the practical benefits of organized cabling. Consider a scenario where a system builder neglects cable management. A tangled mess of cables can obstruct airflow, leading to higher temperatures and potential system instability. Furthermore, if a component needs to be replaced, the tangled cables can make it difficult to access the component and can increase the risk of accidentally damaging other parts during the replacement process. A well-managed cabling system, on the other hand, allows for easy access to components and facilitates efficient airflow, contributing to a cooler and more reliable system. Therefore, taking the time to properly manage cables during PC assembly is a worthwhile investment that pays off in improved system performance, easier maintenance, and a cleaner, more professional-looking build.

3.4 COMPONENT INSTALLATION AND CONFIGURATION (BIOS/UEFI SETTINGS)

Following the physical assembly of a PC, the BIOS (Basic Input/Output System) or its modern successor, UEFI (Unified Extensible Firmware Interface), requires configuration to ensure the system boots correctly and operates as intended. The BIOS/UEFI is a low-level firmware residing on a chip on the motherboard. It plays a crucial role in initializing the hardware components during the boot-up process, performing a Power-On Self-Test (POST) to verify the functionality of connected devices. Beyond basic hardware initialization, the BIOS/UEFI provides a user interface for configuring various system settings. These settings include the boot order, which determines the sequence in which the computer attempts to boot from different devices (hard drives, SSDs, USB drives, DVD drives). Setting the correct boot order is essential for installing an operating system from a USB drive or DVD. Other configurable settings include the system date and time, fan speeds, and advanced options like CPU overclocking and memory timings. Accessing the

BIOS/UEFI setup utility is typically done by pressing a specific key during the early stages of the boot process. Common keys include Del, F2, F10, F12, or Esc, but the specific key varies depending on the motherboard manufacturer. Consulting the motherboard manual is the most reliable way to determine the correct key. As Mueller (2017) explains, "The BIOS/UEFI is responsible for the initial startup of the computer and provides a way to configure system settings" (p. 257). This underscores the importance of understanding and configuring these settings. A common issue faced by beginners is forgetting to set the boot order to the installation media (USB drive or DVD) when attempting to install an operating system. If the boot order is not correctly configured, the computer will likely attempt to boot from the default boot device, usually the hard drive or SSD, and if no operating system is installed there, it can lead to an error message or a failed boot attempt. Consider a scenario where a user is building a new PC and wants to install Windows from a USB drive. They have correctly assembled the hardware, but they forget to change the boot order in the BIOS/UEFI to prioritize the USB drive. As a result, the computer will likely skip the USB drive and attempt to boot from the (empty) hard drive, preventing the Windows installation process from beginning. To resolve this, the user needs to access the BIOS/UEFI setup utility, navigate to the boot order settings (often found under a "Boot" or "Boot Order" tab), and change the priority to place the USB drive at the top of the list. Saving the changes and exiting the BIOS/UEFI will then allow the computer to boot from the USB drive and begin the operating system installation. Therefore, understanding the role of the BIOS/UEFI and how to configure its settings is a crucial step in the PC assembly process. It's not just about getting the hardware together; it's about configuring the system to work correctly and enabling it to load and run the operating system.

3.5 PC Disassembly Procedures

Disassembling a PC, while seemingly the reverse of the assembly process, requires just as much care and attention to detail to prevent damage to components and ensure a smooth process. A crucial first step, and one that should never be overlooked, is disconnecting the power supply from the wall outlet and, ideally, discharging any residual power by holding down the power button for a few seconds. This simple step prevents accidental electrical shocks and protects sensitive components from damage. All cables connected to the system unit, including power cables, data cables, and peripheral connections, should be carefully disconnected and labeled if necessary to facilitate reassembly. The disassembly process should proceed systematically, starting with the easiest components to remove, such as the side panels of the case. Expansion cards, like graphics cards or network cards, are then removed from their respective slots on the motherboard, taking care to release any retaining clips or screws. Storage devices, including HDDs and SSDs, are then detached from their bays, followed by the power supply unit. The more complex components, such as the CPU and motherboard, should be removed last. When removing the CPU, extreme caution is necessary to avoid bending the delicate pins. The CPU cooler must be detached first, and then the CPU retaining mechanism on the socket should be released before carefully lifting the CPU. All removed components, especially electronic ones, should be stored in anti-static bags to protect them from ESD. Keeping track of all screws, standoffs, and small parts is essential to avoid losing them and to ensure a smooth reassembly process. A magnetic parts tray can be invaluable for this purpose. As Mueller (2017) advises, "Disassembly should be performed in a careful and methodical manner to avoid damaging components" (p. 278). This highlights the importance of a structured approach. A common mistake, particularly among those inexperienced with PC disassembly, is trying to force components out of their sockets or slots. If a component doesn't come out easily, it's crucial to stop and double-check that all screws, latches, and retaining mechanisms have been released. Applying excessive force can easily damage components or even the motherboard itself. Consider a technician disassembling a laptop for repair. They might need to remove the display assembly to access internal components. If they try to force the display off without properly disconnecting the cables and releasing the latches, they risk breaking the display or damaging the connectors. A more methodical approach, following the laptop's service manual and taking the time to carefully disconnect all connections, will prevent damage and ensure a successful disassembly. Therefore, understanding the correct PC disassembly procedures is essential for anyone working with computer hardware. It's not just about taking the machine apart; it's about doing so safely and efficiently, preserving the integrity of the components and facilitating future repairs or upgrades.

CHAPTER 4

PREVENTIVE

MAINTENANCE AND

TROUBLESHOOTING

Maintaining a computer system is an ongoing process that involves both proactive preventive measures and reactive troubleshooting skills. Preventive maintenance aims to keep the system running smoothly and efficiently, minimizing the risk of unexpected failures and extending the lifespan of the hardware. Troubleshooting, on the other hand, focuses on diagnosing and resolving problems when they occur, restoring the system to proper working order. This section will delve into the importance of preventive maintenance, outlining effective strategies and best practices, discuss various troubleshooting techniques for identifying and resolving hardware and software issues, and examine some common hardware problems and their corresponding solutions. Consider a large organization relying on a network of computers for its daily operations. Implementing a robust preventive maintenance schedule, including regular software updates, hardware cleaning, and data backups, can significantly reduce the risk of system downtime and data loss, ensuring business continuity. Conversely, when a computer malfunctions, a skilled technician with effective troubleshooting abilities can quickly diagnose the problem, whether it's a software conflict or a hardware failure, and implement the necessary repairs, minimizing disruption to the organization's workflow. As Stallings (2018) explains, "System maintenance is an essential aspect of computer system management" (p. 315). This emphasizes the ongoing nature of maintaining computer systems. A common question is why preventive maintenance is so important. The answer is that it helps to prevent problems before they occur, saving time, money, and frustration in the long run. Regular cleaning of dust buildup, for example, can prevent overheating and extend the life of components. Regular software updates patch security vulnerabilities and improve system stability. Regular data backups protect against data loss in the event of a hardware failure. Troubleshooting skills are equally important. When a problem arises, a systematic approach is crucial. This often involves gathering information about the problem, identifying potential causes, testing hypotheses, and implementing solutions. Consider a scenario where a user's computer is running slowly. A systematic troubleshooting approach might involve checking for resource-intensive processes, scanning for malware, checking hard drive health, and updating drivers. If the problem persists, more advanced troubleshooting techniques, such as checking system logs or using diagnostic tools, might be necessary. Therefore, a combination of proactive preventive maintenance and effective troubleshooting skills is essential for ensuring the smooth and reliable operation of computer systems. It's not just about fixing problems when they occur; it's about preventing them in the first place and having the skills to diagnose and resolve issues quickly and efficiently when they do arise.

4.1 IMPORTANCE OF PREVENTIVE MAINTENANCE

Preventive maintenance is not merely a good practice; it's a crucial necessity for ensuring the longevity, stability, and optimal performance of any computer system, regardless of its age. Just as a car requires regular servicing to maintain its performance and prevent breakdowns, a computer system benefits significantly from routine checks and upkeep. Think of preventive maintenance as an investment in the long-term health of your computer. It's about proactively identifying potential problems before they escalate into major failures, minimizing downtime, and extending the lifespan of valuable hardware components. Regular maintenance also contributes to a more stable and secure computing environment, reducing the risk of data loss, system crashes, and security breaches. For example, regularly cleaning dust from inside the system unit, a seemingly simple task, is vital for preventing overheating, a leading cause of hardware failure. Dust buildup acts as an insulator, trapping heat and preventing components from cooling effectively. As Muller (2017) explains, "Overheating is a major cause of premature component failure" (p.

345). Regular cleaning, using compressed air or a soft brush, ensures proper airflow and helps keep components within their safe operating temperature range. A common misconception is that preventive maintenance is only necessary for older computers that are showing signs of wear and tear. In reality, even brand-new systems benefit from regular checks and maintenance. New systems are not immune to issues like software conflicts, driver problems, or even early hardware failures. Regularly updating software, including the operating system and drivers, is essential for patching security vulnerabilities and ensuring compatibility between hardware and software. Similarly, performing regular system scans for malware and viruses helps to protect against security threats and maintain system stability. Consider a professional photographer who relies on their computer for editing and storing valuable images. Implementing a preventive maintenance schedule, including regular data backups, software updates, and hardware checks, is crucial for protecting their work and ensuring they can continue to operate without interruption. Losing data due to a hard drive failure or experiencing system crashes during a critical project could have significant consequences. Therefore, preventive maintenance is not just about keeping older computers running; it's about ensuring the reliability, security, and performance of *all* computer systems, regardless of their age. It's a proactive approach that minimizes the risk of problems, reduces downtime, and protects valuable data, ultimately saving time, money, and frustration in the long run.

4.2 CLEANING PROCEDURES

Dust accumulation is a significant threat to the health and performance of computer hardware. Like plaque buildup in arteries, dust acts as an insulator, trapping heat and preventing components from cooling effectively. This can lead to overheating, which, as previously discussed, is a major cause of premature component failure. Dust can also clog fans, reducing their efficiency and further exacerbating the heat problem. Therefore, regular cleaning is not just a cosmetic exercise; it's an essential part of preventive maintenance. Compressed air is the most effective tool for removing dust from inside the system unit. Canned compressed air, readily available at most electronics stores, provides a focused and controlled blast of air to dislodge dust from even the most hard-to-reach areas. Avoid using a traditional vacuum cleaner inside the system unit. While it might seem like a convenient option, vacuum cleaners can generate significant static electricity, posing a risk of ESD damage to sensitive components. Furthermore, the suction from a vacuum cleaner can be too strong for delicate parts, potentially dislodging components or damaging connectors. For cleaning external surfaces, such as the case or keyboard, a soft, slightly damp cloth is ideal. Ensure the cloth is not dripping wet, as excess moisture can be harmful to electronic components. Before cleaning any part of the computer, it's absolutely crucial to power off the system and unplug it from the wall outlet. This prevents accidental electrical shocks and protects the hardware from damage. As Mueller (2017) advises, "Regular cleaning is essential for preventing overheating and extending the life of components" (p. 367). This highlights the direct link between cleaning and hardware longevity. A common question is how often cleaning should be performed. The frequency depends largely on the environment in which the computer operates. Computers in dusty or smoky environments will naturally require more frequent cleaning than those in cleaner settings. Generally, cleaning every three to six months is a good practice for most users. Consider a computer used in a workshop or a home with pets. These environments tend to have higher levels of dust and airborne particles, necessitating more frequent cleaning, perhaps every month or two. On the other hand, a computer in a relatively clean office environment might only need cleaning every six months. Another real-world example is a server room in a data center. These environments are typically kept very clean to minimize dust accumulation, but even there, regular cleaning schedules are in place to ensure optimal performance and prevent hardware failures. Therefore, understanding the importance of regular cleaning, using the appropriate tools and techniques, and tailoring the cleaning schedule to the specific environment are all essential aspects of preventive maintenance for computer systems. It's a relatively simple task that can have a significant impact on the reliability and longevity of computer hardware.

4.3 SOFTWARE MAINTENANCE (UPDATES, BACKUPS)

Software maintenance is an equally crucial aspect of computer system upkeep as hardware maintenance, often overlooked but essential for ensuring smooth operation, security, and data integrity. Keeping software updated is not simply about having the latest bells and whistles; it's primarily about patching security vulnerabilities that can be exploited by malicious actors. Software updates also often include performance improvements, bug fixes, and compatibility enhancements, contributing to a more stable and efficient computing experience. Regularly backing up important data is absolutely critical. Data loss can occur due to a multitude of reasons, including hardware failure (hard drive crashes), software corruption, accidental deletion, or even theft. Without regular backups, valuable files, documents, photos, and other data can be irretrievably lost. A reliable backup solution is essential, and this might involve a combination of strategies. External hard drives provide a local backup option, offering relatively fast data transfer speeds and easy access to backed-up files. Cloud storage services offer offsite backups, protecting data from physical damage to the primary storage location and providing access to files from anywhere with an internet connection. A hybrid approach, combining local and offsite backups, offers the best of both worlds, providing both speed and redundancy. As Silberschatz et al. (2018) discuss, "Data backup and recovery are essential aspects of system administration" (p. 456). This underscores the importance of data protection in any computing environment. A common and dangerous mistake is neglecting to back up data until a problem occurs. Waiting until a hard drive fails or files are accidentally deleted is too late. Regular backups should be a routine part of computer maintenance, performed on a schedule that matches the importance of the data and the frequency of changes. Consider a small business that relies on its computers for storing customer data, financial records, and other critical information. Implementing a regular backup schedule, perhaps daily or weekly, using both an external hard drive and a cloud backup service, is crucial for protecting this data. In the event of a hardware failure or a ransomware attack, the business can restore its data from the backups and continue operations with minimal disruption. Another real-world example is a software developer working on a large project. Regularly backing up their code repository to a version control system (like Git) and an offsite server is essential for protecting their work from accidental deletion, hardware failure, or even collaboration issues. Therefore, software maintenance, including regular updates and consistent data backups, is a non-negotiable aspect of computer system management. It's not just about keeping the software running smoothly; it's about protecting valuable data, ensuring system security, and minimizing the impact of unexpected problems. Developing a robust backup strategy and adhering to a regular update schedule are essential practices for any computer user, from individuals to large organizations.

4.4 TROUBLESHOOTING TECHNIQUES (SYSTEMATIC APPROACH)

Troubleshooting computer problems, a skill honed through experience and practice, necessitates a systematic and methodical approach to effectively diagnose and resolve issues. Rushing to conclusions without proper investigation can often lead to misdiagnosis and wasted time. The first crucial step in any troubleshooting process is gathering comprehensive information about the problem. This involves asking key questions: What exactly happened? When did the problem start? What were you doing when the problem occurred? These seemingly simple questions provide valuable context and can offer clues to the underlying cause. The next step is attempting to reproduce the problem. Reproducibility is key to understanding the issue and confirming whether a proposed solution is effective. If the problem can be consistently reproduced, it becomes much easier to isolate the root cause. Once a clear understanding of the problem is established, begin with the simplest and most obvious solutions first. Check all physical connections, ensuring cables are securely plugged in. A simple restart of the computer can often resolve transient software glitches or temporary resource conflicts. Running built-in diagnostic tools, such as memory checkers or disk scanners, can help identify hardware problems. If the problem persists after these initial steps, more advanced troubleshooting techniques are required. Checking device drivers for updates or conflicts is a common next step. Examining system logs, event viewers on Windows or system logs on Linux/macOS, can provide detailed information about system events and errors, often pinpointing the source of the problem. Searching online forums and knowledge bases for similar issues can often lead to solutions or insights from other users who have encountered the same problem. As Mueller (2017) emphasizes, "A systematic approach is essential for effective troubleshooting" (p. 405). This systematic approach often involves a process of elimination, where potential causes are systematically ruled out until the actual cause is identified. A common pitfall in troubleshooting is jumping to conclusions without thoroughly investigating the problem. For instance, a user experiencing slow internet browsing might immediately suspect a problem with their internet service provider. However, the actual problem could be a misconfigured browser, a malware infection, or even a faulty network cable. A systematic approach would involve checking the network connection locally, testing other devices on the same network, scanning for malware, and checking browser settings before contacting the ISP. Consider a scenario where a computer is displaying a blue screen of death (BSOD). This can be a daunting issue, but a systematic approach is crucial. The technician might start by noting the error message displayed on the BSOD, which can provide clues to the problem. They might then try booting the computer in safe mode to see if the problem persists. They might also check recent software installations or hardware changes that could have triggered the BSOD. System logs would be invaluable in this situation, often providing detailed information about the events leading up to the crash. Therefore, developing strong troubleshooting skills, including the ability to gather information, reproduce problems, and systematically test potential solutions, is essential for any computer professional. It's a skill that requires patience, persistence, and a logical mindset, but it is crucial for keeping computer systems running smoothly and efficiently.

4.5 COMMON HARDWARE PROBLEMS AND SOLUTIONS

Computer systems, despite their increasing reliability, are still susceptible to a range of hardware problems. Understanding common symptoms and their potential causes is essential for effective troubleshooting and timely resolution. Boot issues, such as the computer not turning on at all or getting stuck at the BIOS/UEFI screen, can stem from several potential culprits. A faulty power supply is a prime suspect, as it's responsible for providing power to all system components. A failing motherboard can also prevent the system from booting, as it's the central hub connecting all the hardware. Other potential causes include a problem with the front panel connectors (power button) or even a simple issue like a power cord not being properly plugged in. Display problems, manifesting as a blank screen, a distorted image, or no signal, can often be traced to a faulty monitor, a malfunctioning graphics card, or a damaged cable connecting the two. It's crucial to test each component individually to isolate the problem. For instance, connecting the monitor to another computer or trying a different cable can help determine if the issue lies with the monitor or the graphics card. Performance issues, such as slow boot times, application crashes, or general system sluggishness, can be attributed to a variety of factors. Insufficient RAM can lead to excessive paging, where the system relies heavily on the much slower hard drive as virtual memory, causing significant slowdowns. A slow hard drive, particularly an aging HDD, can also contribute to slow boot times and application loading. Overheating, as discussed earlier, can cause components to throttle their performance to reduce heat generation, leading to noticeable slowdowns and even system instability. As Mueller (2017) explains, "Understanding common hardware problems and their solutions is crucial for effective troubleshooting" (p. 425). This knowledge is the foundation of efficient diagnosis. A series of beeps during boot-up, often referred to as "beep codes," can provide valuable clues to the nature of the hardware problem. These beep codes are standardized to some extent, and consulting the motherboard manual is essential for deciphering their meaning. For example, a specific sequence of beeps might indicate a problem with the RAM, the graphics card, or the CPU. Consider a scenario where a user's computer is experiencing intermittent crashes. A systematic approach would involve checking system logs for error messages, monitoring CPU and GPU temperatures, testing the RAM with a memory diagnostic tool, and checking the hard drive for errors. If the system logs indicate a driver issue, updating or reinstalling the relevant driver might resolve the problem. If the temperatures are excessively high, improving cooling, perhaps by cleaning dust or adding more fans, could be the solution. Therefore, understanding common hardware problems, their associated symptoms, and effective troubleshooting techniques is a crucial skill for anyone working with computer systems. It's a combination of knowledge, systematic investigation, and a process of elimination that leads to efficient and accurate diagnoses.

4.6 USING DIAGNOSTIC TOOLS (MEMORY TESTERS, MULTIMETERS)

Diagnostic tools are invaluable assets in the troubleshooting process, providing concrete data and insights that can pinpoint hardware problems with greater accuracy than relying solely on observation and deduction. These tools offer a more objective approach, allowing technicians to verify suspicions and isolate faulty components efficiently. Memory testers, such as the widely used Memtest86, are specifically designed to check for errors in RAM modules. RAM issues can manifest in various ways, from system crashes and data corruption to seemingly random application errors. Memtest86 runs independently of the operating system, directly testing the RAM for any inconsistencies or failures. This makes it a powerful tool for diagnosing memory-related problems that might not be apparent during normal system operation. Multimeters, versatile electronic measuring instruments, are essential for testing power supply voltages and checking for continuity in cables. A multimeter can verify whether the power supply is delivering the correct voltages to the various components, ruling out a faulty power supply as the source of the problem. Checking for continuity in cables ensures that there are no breaks or shorts in the wiring, which can cause intermittent connectivity issues or complete device failure. As Horowitz and Hill (2015) explain, "Test equipment is essential for diagnosing and repairing electronic systems" (p. 823). This underscores the importance of using specialized tools for effective troubleshooting. A common question is when to use diagnostic tools. They are most effective when other, simpler troubleshooting steps have failed to identify the root cause. For example, if a computer is experiencing frequent blue screen errors, and basic checks like driver updates and system file checks haven't resolved the issue, running a memory test with Memtest86 would be the next logical step. Similarly, if a peripheral device is not working, and the connection seems secure, using a multimeter to check the cable for continuity and the power supply for correct voltage output can help isolate the problem. Consider a scenario where a technician is troubleshooting a computer that intermittently freezes. The symptoms suggest a potential memory issue. Instead of simply replacing the RAM modules, which can be costly and time-consuming, the technician can use Memtest86 to thoroughly test the existing RAM. If Memtest86 reports errors, it confirms the RAM as the problem, allowing the technician to replace the faulty modules with confidence. If the test passes, the technician can then focus on other potential causes, saving time and resources. Another real-world example is a network administrator diagnosing connectivity issues on a network segment. Using a network cable tester, a specialized type of multimeter, they can check the cables for proper wiring and continuity, quickly identifying any faulty cables that might be disrupting network communication. Therefore, understanding the functionalities of diagnostic tools like memory testers and multimeters, and knowing when and how to use them, is essential for any computer technician or system administrator. These tools provide valuable data that takes the guesswork out of troubleshooting, leading to faster and more accurate diagnoses, and ultimately, more effective solutions.

CHAPTER 5

OPERATING SYSTEMS

AND SOFTWARE

The operating system (OS) serves as the fundamental software layer that acts as an intermediary between the computer hardware and the user, effectively managing system resources and providing a platform upon which all other applications can run. It's the conductor of the hardware orchestra, allocating resources like CPU time, memory, and storage to different programs, ensuring they can function harmoniously. A deep understanding of OS fundamentals, including process management, memory management, file systems, and I/O handling, is essential for anyone working with computer systems, from software developers crafting applications to system administrators managing complex server infrastructures. Beyond the core OS concepts, understanding software installation procedures, driver management, and security best practices are also crucial for maintaining a stable and secure computing environment. Consider a scenario where a software developer is creating a new application.

They need to understand how the OS manages processes and memory to write efficient code that utilizes system resources effectively. They also need to be aware of the different file systems supported by the OS to ensure their application can store and retrieve data correctly. Similarly, a system administrator managing a network of servers needs to be proficient in OS administration tasks, such as user management, security configuration, and performance tuning. They need to understand how the OS interacts with the underlying hardware to optimize server performance and ensure system stability. As Silberschatz et al. (2018) explain, "An operating system is the fundamental software that manages the computer's hardware and software resources and provides a basis for application programs" (p. 3). This definition highlights the OS's central role in the computer system. A common question is why understanding operating systems is so important, even for someone primarily focused on application development. The answer is that software and hardware are inextricably linked. Software is designed to run on specific operating systems, and understanding the OS's capabilities and limitations is essential for writing efficient and reliable code. Furthermore, many software development tasks, such as debugging and performance optimization, require a deep understanding of how the OS interacts with the hardware. Consider a scenario where a user is experiencing slow performance on their computer. Troubleshooting this issue might involve examining the OS's task manager to identify resource-intensive processes, checking for driver updates, or even analyzing system logs for errors. A solid understanding of OS concepts is essential for effectively diagnosing and resolving such problems. Therefore, a strong foundation in operating system principles, coupled with practical skills in software installation, driver management, and security practices, is essential for anyone seeking a career in computer science or IT. It's the bridge that connects the world of hardware to the realm of software, enabling us to harness the power of computing effectively.

5.1 OPERATING SYSTEM FUNDAMENTALS

The operating system (OS) forms the very foundation of a computer system, acting as the central software entity that exerts control over all aspects of its operation. It's more than just a collection of programs; it's the essential layer that manages the computer's resources, including the CPU, memory (RAM), storage devices (HDDs, SSDs), and peripheral devices (keyboards, mice, printers, etc.). Crucially, the OS provides a consistent and abstracted interface for applications to interact with the underlying hardware. Without this abstraction, application developers would need to write code that is intimately tied to the specific hardware configuration of each machine, a practically impossible task. The OS shields applications from these hardware complexities, providing a set of well-defined services that applications can use to perform tasks like reading and writing files, displaying output on the screen, or communicating over a network. Consider a word processing application. The application doesn't need to know the specific details of how the hard drive stores data or how the monitor displays text. It simply makes requests to the OS, which then handles the low-level interactions with the hardware. This abstraction simplifies application development significantly, allowing developers to focus on the application's functionality rather than hardware specifics. As Tanenbaum and Bos (2015) explain, "The operating system is the software that makes the computer usable" (p. 2). This usability stems from the OS's role as a resource manager and abstraction layer. A common question is why different operating systems exist (Windows, macOS, Linux, etc.). The answer lies in the different design philosophies, target hardware platforms, and user needs that these operating systems address. Each OS has its own kernel, the core of the OS that directly interacts with the hardware, and its own set of system utilities and applications. For instance, Windows is widely used on personal computers due to its broad software compatibility and user-friendly interface. macOS is tailored for Apple's hardware and emphasizes a consistent user experience across its ecosystem. Linux, an open-source OS, is highly versatile and used in a wide range of devices, from embedded systems to supercomputers, due to its flexibility and customizability. Consider a large data center running a complex database application. The data center might choose a Linux distribution for its server operating system due to its stability, performance, and extensive support for server-related software. The system administrators would interact with the Linux OS through command-line interfaces and configuration files to manage the database server and other system services. Therefore, understanding the fundamental role of the operating system as a resource manager, abstraction layer, and platform for applications is essential for any computer scientist or IT professional. The OS is the foundation upon which all other software is built, and its design and functionality have a profound impact on the overall performance, security, and usability of a computer system.

5.1.1 Types of Operating Systems

The landscape of operating systems (OSs) is diverse, with several options available, each possessing unique strengths and weaknesses tailored to specific needs and use cases. Windows, developed by Microsoft, dominates the desktop OS market, renowned for its user-friendly interface, broad software compatibility, and extensive hardware support. Its widespread adoption makes it a familiar environment for most users, and its large software ecosystem ensures compatibility with a vast array of applications, from productivity suites to games. macOS, Apple's operating system, is tightly coupled with Apple's hardware ecosystem, known for its elegant design, intuitive user experience, and strong focus on creative applications. Its emphasis on seamless integration between hardware and software makes it a popular choice among creative professionals and Apple enthusiasts. Linux, an open-source operating system, stands out for its flexibility, customizability, and robust command-line interface. Its open-source nature allows for community-driven development and a wide range of distributions (e.g., Ubuntu, Fedora, CentOS), each tailored for different purposes. Linux is a popular choice among developers, system administrators, and users who appreciate its control and customizability. Beyond these common desktop OSs, specialized operating systems exist for a variety of devices and applications. Embedded systems, found in devices like cars, appliances, and industrial equipment, often run real-time operating systems (RTOSs) designed for specific tasks and resource constraints. Mobile devices, such as smartphones and tablets, utilize mobile operating systems like Android (based on Linux) and iOS, optimized for touch interfaces and mobile hardware. Mainframes, large, powerful computers used in enterprise environments, often run specialized operating systems designed for high transaction volumes and reliability. As Tanenbaum and Bos (2015) explain, "The choice of operating system depends on the user's needs and the hardware being used" (p. 15). This highlights the crucial relationship between the OS and its intended use case. A common question is which OS is "best." There's no single "best" OS; the optimal choice depends entirely on the user's individual needs, preferences, and the tasks they intend to perform. Windows remains a strong choice for general-purpose computing, gaming, and users who require compatibility with a wide range of software. macOS is a compelling option for creative professionals, Apple users, and those who prioritize design and user experience. Linux is often the preferred choice for server applications, software development, and users who value flexibility, control, and open-source software. Consider a software development company building a web application. They might choose Linux for their development servers due to its stability, command-line tools, and cost-effectiveness. Their developers might use macOS or Windows on their personal workstations, depending on their individual preferences and the specific development tools they use. Therefore, understanding the strengths and weaknesses of different operating systems is essential for making informed decisions about which OS best suits a particular use case. The choice is rarely simple and often involves considering factors like software compatibility, hardware requirements, user familiarity, cost, and the specific tasks the OS will be used for.

5.1.2 OS Installation and Configuration

Installing and configuring an operating system (OS) is a fundamental skill for any computer professional or enthusiast, involving a series of steps that prepare the hardware for software operation. The installation process typically begins with partitioning the hard drive, dividing it into logical sections for the OS and other data. This partitioning allows for organizing files and even dual-booting multiple operating systems on the same drive. Next, the OS files are copied from the installation media (USB drive, DVD, or network share) to the designated partition on the hard drive. This process lays the foundation for the OS to function. After the files are copied, the OS installation proceeds with configuring system settings, including setting up user accounts, configuring network settings (IP address, DNS), and installing necessary hardware drivers. Drivers are essential software components that allow the OS to communicate with specific hardware devices, ensuring they function correctly. The specific steps and options available during installation and configuration vary slightly depending on the OS (Windows, macOS, Linux), but the general principles of partitioning, file copying, and system configuration remain similar. As Silberschatz et al. (2018) explain, "The installation process involves loading the kernel into memory and configuring the operating system" (p. 56). This highlights the transition from the initial boot process to the fully functional OS. A common challenge encountered, especially by beginners, is troubleshooting boot problems after a failed OS installation. These problems can manifest in various ways, such as the computer getting stuck at the boot screen, displaying error messages, or simply refusing to boot at all. Booting from the original installation media and using the OS's built-in repair tools is often the most effective way to resolve these issues. These repair tools can automatically diagnose and fix common boot problems, such as corrupted boot sectors, missing system files, or incorrect boot configurations. Consider a scenario where a user is attempting to install a new version of Windows. They encounter a problem during the installation process, and the computer now refuses to boot. Booting from the Windows installation USB drive and selecting the "Repair your computer" option provides access to tools like Startup Repair, which can automatically fix common boot problems. If the automatic repair fails, more advanced options like using the command prompt to manually repair the boot configuration files might be necessary. Another real-world example is a system administrator setting up a new server. After installing the server operating system, they need to configure network settings, install necessary drivers for the server hardware (RAID controllers, network adapters), and set up user accounts and permissions. This configuration process is crucial for ensuring the server functions correctly within the network environment. Therefore, understanding the OS installation and configuration process, including troubleshooting common boot problems, is an essential skill for anyone working with computer systems. It's not just about getting the OS installed; it's about configuring it correctly to meet the user's needs and ensuring it can boot reliably.

5.1.3 File Systems and Disk Management

File systems are the backbone of data organization and management on storage devices, providing the structure and rules that govern how files are stored, accessed, and managed. They act as an intermediary between the operating system and the physical storage hardware, translating file names and directory structures into the physical locations of data on the disk. Different file systems exist, each with its own characteristics and strengths. NTFS (New Technology File System), developed by Microsoft, is the standard file system for Windows, offering features like file permissions, encryption, and journaling for data integrity. APFS (Apple File System) is Apple's modern file system for macOS, designed for performance, security, and efficiency on SSDs and other storage devices. ext4 (Fourth Extended File System) is a widely used file system in the Linux world, known for its stability, performance, and support for large file sizes. Understanding the nuances of these file systems, including their capabilities and limitations, is crucial for system administrators and developers working with different operating system environments. Disk management tools provide a user interface for interacting with storage devices, allowing users to partition hard drives (dividing them into logical volumes), format volumes (preparing them for use with a specific file system), and perform other disk-related tasks. Partitioning allows for organizing data and even dual-booting multiple operating systems on a single drive. Formatting creates the file system structure on a volume, making it ready for storing files. As Silberschatz et al. (2018) explain, "A file system is responsible for organizing and managing files" (p. 256). This organization is critical for efficient data retrieval and storage. A common misconception is that deleting a file permanently removes it from the hard drive. In reality, the file is often just marked as deleted by the file system, and its space on the disk is made available for reuse. The actual data may still be recoverable using specialized data recovery software until it is overwritten by new data. This is why secure deletion methods, which involve overwriting the data multiple times, are necessary for truly erasing sensitive information. Consider a scenario where a user accidentally deletes an important document. They might be able to recover the file using data recovery software if it hasn't been overwritten yet. However, if they need to ensure the file is permanently deleted, they would need to use a secure deletion tool. Another real-world example is a system administrator managing a server with multiple hard drives. They would use disk management tools to configure RAID arrays for data redundancy and performance, creating logical volumes from the physical drives and formatting them with the appropriate file system for the server's applications. Therefore, a thorough understanding of file systems and disk management is essential for anyone working with computer systems. It's not just about storing files; it's about understanding how data is organized and managed on storage devices, how to optimize storage usage, and how to protect data from accidental deletion or unauthorized access.

5.2 DEVICE DRIVERS

Device drivers are essential software programs that act as translators between the operating system (OS) and the various hardware devices connected to a computer system. They bridge the communication gap, allowing the OS to understand and interact with the specific hardware, whether it's a graphics card, a network adapter, a printer, or a USB device. Each hardware device, due to its unique design and functionality, requires a corresponding driver to function correctly. The driver provides the OS with the necessary instructions and protocols to communicate with the device, enabling the OS to send commands and receive data. Without the correct driver, the OS would be unable to recognize or utilize the hardware, rendering the device useless. Think of a newly installed printer. The OS doesn't inherently know how to communicate with that specific printer model. The printer driver provides the OS with the necessary information, such as the printer's capabilities, its communication protocol, and how to send print jobs. Once the driver is installed, the OS can seamlessly interact with the printer, allowing applications to send print commands and users to print documents. As Tanenbaum and Bos

(2015) explain, "Device drivers are software modules that manage particular hardware devices" (p. 287). This management includes handling data transfers, responding to device interrupts, and configuring device settings. A common question is why device drivers are necessary. The answer lies in the vast diversity of hardware devices available. It would be impractical for the OS to include built-in support for every possible hardware configuration. Device drivers provide a modular and extensible way to add support for new devices without requiring changes to the core OS. Consider a scenario where a user upgrades their graphics card. The new graphics card, even from the same manufacturer, likely requires a different driver than the old card. The user needs to install the updated driver for the new card to function correctly with the OS and to take advantage of its features and performance enhancements. Another real-world example is a system administrator setting up a new server with specialized network adapters. The server OS needs the appropriate drivers for these network adapters to communicate on the network and handle network traffic efficiently. Without the correct drivers, the server would be unable to connect to the network, rendering it effectively useless. Therefore, understanding the role and importance of device drivers is essential for anyone working with computer systems. Ensuring that the correct drivers are installed for all hardware devices is crucial for system stability, performance, and functionality. Driver management, including updating drivers to the latest versions and troubleshooting driver conflicts, is a common task for system administrators and IT professionals.

5.2.1 Driver Installation and Updates

Driver installation and updates are crucial aspects of maintaining a healthy and functional computer system. Drivers, as the software intermediaries between the operating system (OS) and hardware devices, are typically provided by the hardware manufacturer. These drivers can be obtained from the manufacturer's website, often available for download, or, in older systems, may have been included on a CD/DVD that came with the hardware. Keeping drivers updated is not merely a matter of convenience; it's essential for maintaining optimal performance, system stability, and, importantly, security. Updated drivers often include performance enhancements, bug fixes, and compatibility improvements, ensuring that the hardware operates at its full potential and interacts seamlessly with the OS. Furthermore, driver updates frequently address security vulnerabilities, patching potential exploits that could be used by malicious actors to compromise the system. In Windows, the Device Manager provides a centralized interface for managing and updating drivers. It allows users to view all connected hardware devices, check driver versions, and initiate driver updates. The Device Manager can also be used to troubleshoot driver-related issues, such as identifying devices with driver problems or rolling back to a previous driver version if a recent update causes instability. As Silberschatz et al. (2018) note, "Device drivers must be installed correctly for the hardware to function properly" (p. 298). This underscores the critical role drivers play in hardware operation. A common issue encountered by users is driver conflicts, which can manifest as system instability, crashes, or device malfunctions. These conflicts can arise when multiple drivers are installed for the same device or when a driver is incompatible with the current OS version. Updating the driver to the latest version is often the first step in resolving such conflicts, as newer versions may include fixes for known compatibility issues. If the latest driver introduces new problems, rolling back to a previously working driver version can be a viable solution. Consider a scenario where a user experiences intermittent system crashes after updating their graphics card driver. Using the Device Manager, they can roll back to the previous driver version, which might resolve the instability. They can then investigate online forums or the graphics card manufacturer's website to determine if others have experienced similar issues with the latest driver and wait for a more stable update before trying again. Another real-world example is a company deploying a new point-of-sale system. Ensuring all devices, from barcode scanners to receipt printers, have the correct and up-to-date drivers is crucial for the system to function reliably. Driver conflicts or outdated drivers can lead to malfunctions, disrupting sales and impacting business operations. Therefore, understanding the importance of driver installation and updates, including how to manage drivers using tools like Device Manager and how to troubleshoot driver conflicts, is essential for anyone working with computer systems. It's not just about getting the hardware to work; it's about ensuring its optimal performance, stability, and security.

5.2.2 Troubleshooting Driver Issues

Troubleshooting driver issues is a common, yet often complex, task faced by computer users and IT professionals. Driver problems can manifest in a variety of ways, from seemingly minor hardware malfunctions, such as a printer refusing to print, to more serious issues like system crashes, blue screens of death (BSODs), or intermittent device disconnections. Effective troubleshooting requires a systematic approach to isolate the problem and implement the appropriate solution. Often, the first step in diagnosing a driver issue involves checking the Device Manager in Windows (or its equivalent in other operating systems). The Device Manager provides a centralized view of all connected hardware devices and often flags devices with driver problems, displaying error messages or warning symbols. These error messages can offer valuable clues about the nature of the driver issue. Updating or reinstalling drivers is a common solution for driver-related problems. Downloading the latest driver from the hardware manufacturer's website is generally recommended, as it often includes bug fixes, performance improvements, and security patches. Reinstalling a driver can also resolve conflicts or corruption issues. Searching online forums and knowledge bases for solutions specific to the hardware and OS version can also be helpful, as other users may have encountered and resolved similar problems. As Tanenbaum and Bos (2015) suggest, "Debugging device drivers can be a challenging task" (p. 302), emphasizing the complexity often associated with driver issues. A common and effective troubleshooting step is to boot the computer in Safe Mode. Safe Mode starts the OS with only essential drivers, disabling most third-party drivers. If the problem disappears in Safe Mode, it strongly suggests that a driver is the culprit. This allows the user to then systematically re-enable drivers one by one to identify the problematic driver. Consider a scenario where a user's computer is experiencing random system crashes. Checking the Device Manager reveals a yellow exclamation mark next to the graphics card, indicating a driver problem. The user then downloads the latest driver from the graphics card manufacturer's website and installs it. If the crashes persist, they might try rolling back to a previous driver version or even uninstalling and reinstalling the driver completely. If these steps fail, booting in Safe Mode can help determine if the graphics card driver is indeed the cause of the crashes. Another real-world example is a company's network printer suddenly stops working. The IT technician might first check the Device Manager on the connected computer to see if the printer driver is reporting any errors. They might then try updating the printer driver or checking the printer manufacturer's website for troubleshooting tips. Booting the computer connected to the printer in Safe Mode can help determine if a conflicting driver or other software issue is interfering with the printer's operation. Therefore, understanding common driver problems, utilizing tools like the Device Manager, and employing systematic troubleshooting steps are essential skills for anyone managing computer systems. It's a process of elimination, often combined with online research and driver updates, to identify and resolve driver-related issues effectively.

5.3 APPLICATION SOFTWARE

Application software constitutes the diverse landscape of programs designed to perform specific tasks, empowering users to interact with computers for a multitude of purposes. These programs, unlike system software like operating systems which manage the computer's core functions, are designed to fulfill specific user needs, ranging from everyday tasks like word processing and web browsing to specialized functions like graphic design, video editing, and scientific computing. Consider a word processing application like Microsoft Word or Google Docs. These programs allow users to create, edit, and format text documents, providing features like spell checking, grammar correction, and document formatting tools. They are essential tools for writing reports, creating presentations, and composing various types of written communication. Web browsers, such as Google Chrome, Mozilla Firefox, or Safari, enable users to access and interact with the World Wide Web, retrieving and displaying web pages, playing online media, and facilitating online communication. They are the gateway to the vast world of information and services available on the internet. Gaming software encompasses a wide range of programs, from simple puzzle games to complex 3D simulations, providing entertainment and often pushing the boundaries of computer hardware capabilities. Beyond these common examples, application software also includes a vast array of specialized programs. Graphic design software, like Adobe Photoshop or Illustrator, empowers users to create and edit digital images. Video editing software, such as Adobe Premiere Pro or Final Cut Pro, allows for the manipulation and editing of video footage. Scientific computing software, like MATLAB or Mathematica, provides tools for performing complex mathematical calculations and simulations. As Tanenbaum and Bos (2015) explain, "Application programs are designed to solve specific user problems" (p. 325). This highlights the user-centric nature of application software. A common question is how to choose the right application software for a specific task. The answer depends on several factors, including the specific requirements of the task, the user's experience level, the budget, and the available hardware. Consider a team of architects using CAD (Computer-Aided Design) software to design a building. They would need specialized CAD software with features tailored to architectural design, such as tools for creating floor plans, modeling 3D structures, and generating building specifications. They would also need computers with sufficient processing power and memory to run the demanding CAD software effectively. Another real-world example is a data scientist using statistical software like R or Python with specialized libraries to analyze large datasets. They would need software with statistical modeling capabilities, data visualization tools, and the ability to handle large datasets efficiently. Therefore, understanding the diverse range of application software available and their specific functionalities is crucial for anyone working with computers. Choosing the right application software can significantly impact productivity, efficiency, and the quality of the work produced. From everyday tasks to complex professional workflows, application software empowers users to leverage the power of computers to achieve their goals.

5.3.1 Types of Applications

Application software, the diverse set of programs designed to perform specific tasks, can be categorized into various types, each catering to different user needs and functionalities. Productivity software, a cornerstone of modern computing, encompasses applications designed to enhance efficiency and streamline workflows. Word processors, like Microsoft Word or Google Docs, facilitate the creation, editing, and formatting of text documents, essential for everything from writing reports to composing emails. Spreadsheets, such as Microsoft Excel or Google Sheets, provide tools for organizing, analyzing, and manipulating numerical data, crucial for financial management, data analysis, and creating charts and graphs. Multimedia software caters to the creation, editing, and playback of various media formats. Video editors, like Adobe Premiere Pro or DaVinci Resolve, enable users to manipulate and edit video footage, creating movies, documentaries, or other video content. Audio players, such as iTunes or VLC, allow for the playback of music and other audio files. Utility software comprises programs designed to maintain and optimize computer systems. Antivirus programs, like Norton or McAfee, protect against malware and other security threats, ensuring system security and data integrity. Disk management tools, such as Disk Defragmenter or file recovery utilities, help manage storage devices, optimize disk performance, and recover lost or deleted files. Games, a significant category of application software, provide entertainment and recreation, ranging from simple puzzle games to complex 3D simulations. The choice of application software is highly dependent on the user's specific needs and the tasks they want to accomplish. As Tanenbaum and Bos (2015) explain, "Application software is designed to solve specific user problems" (p. 325). This user-centric design is what distinguishes application software from system software. A common question is how to choose the right application for a specific task. The answer depends on several factors, including the specific features required, the user's experience level, the budget, and the available hardware. Consider a marketing team collaborating on a project. They might use project management software, like Asana or Trello, to track tasks, assign responsibilities, and manage deadlines. They might also use graphic design software, like Canva or Adobe Photoshop, to create marketing materials. Their choice of software would depend on their specific needs, budget, and the complexity of the project. Another real-world example is a scientist analyzing data from an experiment. They might use statistical software, like R or SPSS, to perform statistical analysis, visualize data, and generate reports. The specific software they choose would depend on the type of data they are analyzing, the statistical methods they need to apply, and their familiarity with different software packages. Therefore, understanding the different categories of application software and their respective functionalities is crucial for effectively utilizing computer systems. Choosing the right application can significantly impact productivity, efficiency, and the quality of the work produced. From everyday tasks to specialized professional workflows, application software empowers users to leverage the power of computers to achieve their goals.

5.3.2 Software Installation and Uninstallation

Software installation and uninstallation are fundamental operations for managing applications on a computer system. Installing software typically involves running an installer program, often provided as an executable file (.exe on Windows, .dmg on macOS, or through package managers on Linux), which guides the user through the process. The installer copies the necessary program files to the appropriate locations on the hard drive, creates necessary directories, and configures the system to recognize and run the newly installed software. This configuration often involves creating registry entries (on Windows) or modifying system configuration files (on other operating systems) to register the application with the OS.

Uninstalling software, conversely, aims to completely remove the program from the system. This involves deleting the program files, removing associated registry entries or configuration settings, and cleaning up any temporary files created during the program's use. Using the OS's built-in uninstallation utility (e.g., "Add/Remove Programs" in older Windows versions, "Programs and Features" in newer Windows versions, or the application uninstaller in macOS) is generally recommended as it attempts to perform a clean removal of the software. As Silberschatz et al. (2018) explain, "Software installation and uninstallation are important tasks in system administration" (p. 356). This highlights the importance of proper software management. A common issue encountered during software uninstallation is leftover files and registry entries. These remnants can clutter the system, consume disk space, and, in some cases, potentially cause conflicts with other applications. Using a dedicated uninstaller tool, often available as a third-party utility, can help address this issue. These specialized tools are designed to thoroughly scan the system for any remaining files, folders, or registry entries associated with the uninstalled program and provide options to remove them. Consider a scenario where a user installs a trial version of a software application.

After the trial period expires, they decide to uninstall the software. Using the standard Windows uninstallation utility might leave behind some files and registry entries, which could interfere with a subsequent installation of a different version of the same software. A dedicated uninstaller tool would help ensure a more thorough removal, preventing potential conflicts. Another real-world example is a system administrator managing a large number of computers. They might use automated software deployment tools to install and uninstall software on multiple machines. These tools often include features for ensuring clean uninstallation, minimizing the risk of leftover files and maintaining system stability. Therefore, understanding the software installation and uninstallation process, including the potential issues of leftover files and the use of dedicated uninstaller tools, is essential for anyone managing computer systems. It's not just about getting the software installed; it's about ensuring proper removal when necessary and maintaining a clean and stable system environment.

5.4 ANTIVIRUS AND SECURITY SOFTWARE

Protecting a computer system from the ever-evolving landscape of malware and other security threats is absolutely crucial in today's interconnected digital world. The consequences of a successful cyberattack can range from minor annoyances to catastrophic data breaches, financial losses, and reputational damage. Robust antivirus and security software are essential tools in mitigating these risks, providing a layered defense against malicious software and unauthorized access. These software solutions typically include features like real-time scanning, which constantly monitors files and system activity for suspicious behavior; scheduled scans, which perform regular checks for malware; and firewall protection, which controls network traffic, blocking unauthorized access to the system. Modern antivirus software goes beyond simply detecting known viruses; it often incorporates heuristic analysis, which identifies potentially malicious behavior even in previously unseen software, and behavioral analysis, which monitors how programs interact with the system to detect suspicious actions. As Stallings (2018) explains,

"Security is a major concern in modern computer systems" (p. 456). This concern is only amplified in today's highly networked environment. A common question is why antivirus software is so important. The answer is that malware, including viruses, worms, trojans, ransomware, and spyware, is constantly evolving, and new threats emerge daily. Without robust protection, computer systems are vulnerable to infection, which can lead to data corruption, system instability, identity theft, and other serious problems. Consider a small business that stores sensitive customer data on its computers. A ransomware attack could encrypt this data, rendering it inaccessible and potentially crippling the business. Having up-to-date antivirus software and a robust backup strategy is essential for mitigating this risk. Another real-world example is a hospital network storing patient medical records. A security breach could compromise this sensitive information, leading to legal liabilities and reputational damage. Strong security software, coupled with other security measures like access controls and regular security audits, is crucial for protecting patient privacy and maintaining the integrity of the medical records. Furthermore, security software is not just about protecting against external threats. It also plays a role in preventing internal threats, such as employees accidentally downloading malware or clicking on phishing links. User education and awareness are also crucial components of a comprehensive security strategy, as even the best security software can be bypassed by careless or uninformed users. Therefore, implementing robust antivirus and security software, combined with user education and a layered security approach, is essential for protecting computer systems from the myriad threats that exist in today's digital landscape. It's an ongoing process that requires constant vigilance and adaptation to the ever-changing threat environment.

5.4.1 Importance of Security

The importance of robust security measures in modern computing cannot be overstated. Malware, encompassing a broad spectrum of malicious software like viruses, worms, ransomware, and spyware, poses a constant and evolving threat to computer systems and the valuable data they hold. These malicious programs can wreak havoc, from corrupting or deleting files and stealing sensitive data like passwords and financial information to disrupting system operations and even holding entire systems hostage through ransomware attacks.

Installing and regularly updating antivirus software is a crucial first line of defense against these threats. Antivirus software scans files and system activity for known malware signatures and suspicious behavior, quarantining or deleting infected files to prevent further damage. However, a common and dangerous misconception is that simply having antivirus software is enough to guarantee complete security. In reality, a multi-layered approach to security is essential, combining technical safeguards with user awareness and responsible computing habits. As Stallings (2018) emphasizes, "Security is not a single product but a set of policies, procedures, and technical measures" (p. 467). This layered approach recognizes that no single solution is foolproof. Strong passwords, regularly changed and unique for each account, are fundamental. They act as the first barrier against unauthorized access. Regular software updates, including the operating system and all applications, are crucial for patching security vulnerabilities that malware can exploit. Safe browsing habits, such as being cautious about clicking on links or downloading files from untrusted sources, are equally important. Phishing attacks, for example, often rely on tricking users into clicking on malicious links or opening infected attachments. A multi-layered approach recognizes that human error can be a weak link in the security chain, and therefore, emphasizes user education and awareness. Consider a scenario where an employee in a company clicks on a phishing email and inadvertently downloads ransomware. Even with antivirus software installed, if the ransomware is new or uses advanced evasion techniques, it could potentially bypass the antivirus scan and encrypt critical company data. A multi-layered approach, including regular data backups and employee training on identifying phishing emails, would be crucial in mitigating the impact of such an attack. Another real-world example is a home user whose computer becomes infected with spyware. The spyware could be silently tracking their online activity, stealing passwords, and even monitoring their keystrokes. While antivirus software might detect some spyware, a combination of strong passwords, regular software updates, and cautious browsing habits would provide a more comprehensive defense. Therefore, understanding the multifaceted nature of security threats and adopting a multi-layered approach is essential for protecting computer systems. It's not just about relying on antivirus software; it's about creating a comprehensive security posture that includes technical safeguards, user education, and responsible computing practices to minimize risks and protect valuable data.

5.4.2 Antivirus Installation and Configuration

Installing and configuring antivirus software is a crucial step in establishing a robust security posture for any computer system. Antivirus software functions by scanning files and programs for known malware signatures, which are unique patterns of code that identify specific malware threats. Upon detecting a known signature, the antivirus software takes action, typically quarantining the infected file to prevent it from running or spreading, or, if possible, removing the malicious code altogether. However, simply installing antivirus software is not enough. Proper configuration is essential to ensure ongoing protection. This includes scheduling regular scans, ideally daily or at least weekly, to check the entire system for malware. Automatic updates are also crucial, as new malware threats are constantly emerging, and the antivirus software needs to have the latest definitions to detect and neutralize them. As Stallings (2018) notes, "Antivirus software must be regularly updated to be effective against new threats" (p. 478). This highlights the dynamic nature of the malware landscape and the need for continuous updates. A common question is which antivirus software is "best." The reality is that several reputable antivirus programs are available, each with its own strengths and weaknesses. The "best" choice often depends on individual needs, preferences, and budget considerations. Some users might prioritize performance and minimal system impact, while others might focus on comprehensive protection and advanced features. Independent testing organizations, such as AV-TEST and AV-Comparatives, regularly evaluate antivirus software and provide comparative reviews, assessing factors like detection rates, performance impact, and usability. These reviews can be a valuable resource for making informed decisions about which antivirus software to choose. Consider a small business owner who needs to protect their office computers from malware. They might consult reviews from AV-TEST or AV-Comparatives to compare different antivirus solutions and choose one that offers a good balance of protection, performance, and cost-effectiveness. They would then configure the chosen software to perform regular scans and automatic updates to ensure ongoing protection. Another real-world example is a home user who primarily uses their computer for web browsing and social media. They might opt for a free antivirus solution that offers basic protection, but they should still ensure it is configured for regular scans and updates. They should also be aware of the limitations of free antivirus software and consider upgrading to a paid version for more comprehensive protection if they handle sensitive data or engage in high-risk online activities. Therefore, understanding the functionality of antivirus software, configuring it correctly for regular scans and updates, and choosing a reputable solution based on individual needs and independent reviews are all essential aspects of computer security. It's not just about installing the software; it's about ensuring it is configured and maintained properly to provide effective protection against the ever-present threat of malware.

5.4.3 Basic Security Practices

While antivirus software provides a crucial layer of defense against malware, it's not a silver bullet for cybersecurity. A comprehensive security posture requires a multi-faceted approach, incorporating various security practices and user awareness to effectively mitigate the diverse range of threats that exist in today's digital landscape.

Using strong and unique passwords for all accounts is fundamental. Strong passwords, characterized by a combination of uppercase and lowercase letters, numbers, and symbols, are more difficult for attackers to crack. Uniqueness is equally important, as using the same password across multiple accounts means that a breach of one account could compromise others. Being cautious about clicking on links or opening attachments from unknown or untrusted sources is another crucial practice. Phishing attacks, a common social engineering tactic, often rely on tricking users into clicking on malicious links or opening infected attachments that can deliver malware or steal sensitive information. Keeping software updated, including the operating system and all applications, is essential for patching security vulnerabilities that attackers can exploit. Software updates often include security fixes that address known vulnerabilities, reducing the risk of compromise. Regularly backing up data is another critical security practice, albeit often overlooked. Backups provide a safety net in case of data loss due to malware attacks, hardware failures, or accidental deletion. As Stallings (2018) emphasizes, "A comprehensive security strategy involves multiple layers of defense" (p. 485). This layered approach recognizes that no single security measure is foolproof. Phishing, as mentioned earlier, is a particularly prevalent threat. It involves tricking users into revealing sensitive information, such as passwords, credit card numbers, or personal details, often through deceptive emails or websites that mimic legitimate ones. Being aware of phishing tactics, such as recognizing suspicious email addresses, hovering over links to check their destination, and being wary of requests for personal information, is crucial for protecting against this type of attack. Consider a scenario where a user receives an email that appears to be from their bank, asking them to verify their account details by clicking on a link. A cautious user would examine the email carefully, noticing perhaps a slightly different sender address or grammatical errors, and would avoid clicking on the link. They might instead contact their bank directly to verify the legitimacy of the email. Another real-world example is a company implementing a security awareness training program for its employees. The training would cover topics like password security, phishing awareness, safe browsing habits, and the importance of keeping software updated. This education empowers employees to be proactive in protecting company data and systems. Therefore, adopting a multi-layered approach to security, including strong passwords, software updates, data backups, and user awareness, is essential for mitigating risks in today's digital environment. It's not just about relying on antivirus software; it's about creating a security-conscious culture and empowering users to make informed decisions that protect themselves and their data.

CHAPTER 6

NETWORKING

FUNDAMENTALS

In our increasingly interconnected world, a solid understanding of networking fundamentals is no longer a luxury but a necessity, even for computer technicians whose primary focus might seem hardware-centric. The ability to diagnose and resolve connectivity issues, understand how computer systems interact within a network, and appreciate the broader context of a computer's role within a larger network infrastructure significantly enhances a technician's capabilities and value. This section provides an overview of basic networking concepts, including network topologies, the physical and logical arrangement of network devices; network devices themselves, like routers, switches, and modems; network addressing, the system used to identify devices on a network; and the principles of wireless networking. While presented as an optional module, mastering these concepts elevates a technician's skillset, enabling them to tackle a wider range of problems and contribute more effectively to complex

IT environments. Consider a scenario where a user reports that their computer can't connect to the internet. A technician with a basic understanding of networking can systematically troubleshoot the issue, checking the physical connections, verifying the IP address configuration, testing the router, and even considering potential DNS problems. Without this fundamental knowledge, the technician might be limited to simply replacing cables or restarting devices, potentially overlooking the actual root cause of the connectivity issue. As Kurose and Ross (2017) explain, "Computer networking is about much more than just connecting computers; it is about enabling communication and resource sharing among a vast array of devices" (p. 2). This highlights the pervasive nature of networking in modern computing. Another real-world example is a technician setting up a small office network. They need to understand how to configure the router, connect the computers and printers to the network, and ensure that all devices can communicate effectively. They might also need to set up a wireless network for mobile devices. A solid grasp of networking concepts is essential for this task. A common question is why a hardware technician needs to understand networking. The answer is that hardware and networking are inextricably linked. Many hardware problems are actually network-related, and a technician who understands networking can diagnose and resolve these issues more effectively. Furthermore, as more and more devices become network-enabled, the lines between hardware and networking are becoming increasingly blurred. Therefore, a solid foundation in networking fundamentals is no longer optional for computer technicians; it's a crucial skill that expands their capabilities, enhances their problem-solving abilities, and prepares them for the increasingly networked world of computing. It empowers them to not just fix computers, but to understand how they function within the larger context of a connected world.

6.1 NETWORK TOPOLOGIES

Network topology refers to the arrangement of devices and connections within a network, defining the physical or logical layout of how data flows between them. It's the architectural blueprint of the network, impacting everything from performance and redundancy to ease of management and cost. Different topologies offer varying levels of these characteristics, making the choice of topology a critical decision in network design. Several fundamental topologies exist, each with its own advantages and disadvantages. A bus topology, historically significant, connects all devices to a single cable or backbone. While simple to implement, a break in the cable can disrupt the entire network. A star topology connects each device to a central hub or switch. This offers greater resilience, as a failure of one connection only affects that specific device, but the central hub becomes a single point of failure. A ring topology connects devices in a circular fashion, with data traveling around the ring. While offering high performance, it can be complex to implement and is vulnerable to single points of failure. A mesh topology connects each device to multiple other devices, providing high redundancy and fault tolerance, but at the cost of increased complexity and cabling. Finally, a tree topology combines elements of star and bus topologies, offering a hierarchical structure. As Kurose and Ross (2017) explain, "Network topology plays a crucial role in determining network performance, reliability, and cost" (p. 157). This highlights the significant impact of topology choices. A common question is which topology is "best." The answer, as with many engineering decisions, depends on the specific requirements of the network. A small home network might opt for a simple star topology using a wireless router, balancing cost-effectiveness and ease of use. A large enterprise network, on the other hand, might employ a more complex mesh or hierarchical topology to ensure high availability and redundancy for critical systems. Consider a data center hosting critical web services. High availability is paramount, so a redundant mesh-like topology, potentially incorporating multiple switches and redundant connections, would be crucial. A failure of a single connection should not disrupt service. Another real-world example is a large office building. A hierarchical tree topology might be employed, with departmental switches connecting to a central router, providing a balance of performance, scalability, and manageability. This allows for isolating network issues

144

to specific departments without affecting the entire network. Therefore, understanding the characteristics of different network topologies is essential for designing and implementing effective networks. The choice of topology is a trade-off between factors like cost, complexity, performance, and redundancy, and it must be carefully considered based on the specific needs of the network and its users.

6.1.1 Star Topology

The star topology has become the dominant network architecture in modern networks, prized for its simplicity, reliability, and ease of management. In this configuration, every device on the network connects directly to a central hub or, more commonly, a switch. This central device acts as the focal point for all network communication, receiving data from any connected device and forwarding it only to the intended recipient. This centralized approach offers significant advantages over older topologies like the bus or ring. One of the primary benefits of the star topology is its ease of installation and troubleshooting. Adding a new device to the network is as simple as connecting it to an available port on the central switch.

145

Troubleshooting is also simplified, as a problem with one device or its connection only affects that specific device; the rest of the network remains operational. If a cable is broken or a device malfunctions, it doesn't bring down the entire network, a critical advantage in today's always-connected world. As Kurose and Ross (2017) explain, "The star topology has become the dominant topology in modern LANs due to its simplicity and reliability" (p. 162). This widespread adoption speaks to the practical benefits of this architecture. A real-world example that is immediately familiar to most users is a typical home network. In this scenario, all computers, smartphones, tablets, and other network-enabled devices connect to a central Wi-Fi router, which acts as the switch. This router, in turn, connects to the internet modem, providing internet access to all connected devices. If one device on the home network malfunctions or is turned off, it does not affect the other devices' ability to connect to the network or access the internet. Consider a small office network. All computers, printers, and other devices are connected to a central switch located in a wiring closet. This switch manages all network traffic within the office, allowing employees to share files, access the internet, and use network-connected peripherals. The star topology ensures that if one

146

employee's computer has a problem, it doesn't disrupt the network connectivity of other employees. Another example is a large corporate network, which, while more complex, still relies heavily on the star topology at the local level. Individual departments or workgroups might connect to departmental switches, which then connect to larger core switches, forming a hierarchical star topology. This structure allows for efficient traffic management and isolates network segments, improving overall network performance and resilience. Therefore, the star topology's ease of use, reliability, and scalability have made it the preferred choice for most modern networks, from small home networks to large enterprise infrastructures. Its centralized design simplifies management and troubleshooting, making it a practical and cost-effective solution for a wide range of networking needs.

6.1.2 Bus Topology

The bus topology, a historically significant network architecture, connects all devices to a single communication line, commonly referred to as the bus. This shared cable acts as the backbone of the network, with all devices "tapping" into it to send and receive data.

While simple to implement in its basic form, the bus topology suffers from a significant vulnerability: a break or fault in the cable disrupts communication for the entire network. Because all devices rely on the single bus for communication, a cable cut effectively brings down the entire network segment. This single point of failure makes the bus topology less desirable for mission-critical applications or environments where network downtime is unacceptable. Data transmission on a bus network typically involves broadcasting, where a device sends data onto the bus, and all other devices "listen" to the bus. Only the device with the intended destination address will actually accept the data; other devices ignore it. This broadcast nature can also lead to performance issues as the number of devices on the bus increases, as collisions can occur when multiple devices try to transmit simultaneously. As Kurose and Ross (2017) explain, "The bus topology's primary disadvantage is its lack of redundancy; a break in the bus cable brings down the entire network" (p. 160). This inherent vulnerability is the main reason why the bus topology has largely fallen out of favor in modern network deployments. A historical example of the bus topology in action is early Ethernet networks, which utilized coaxial cable as the bus. These early Ethernet networks were relatively simple to set up, but they were susceptible to cable breaks and performance degradation as the network grew. Terminators were required at each end of the coaxial cable to prevent signal reflections, which could interfere with network communication. Consider a small office using an early Ethernet network with a bus topology. If a cable is accidentally cut or damaged, the entire office network would be disrupted, preventing employees from accessing the internet, sharing files, or using network printers. Troubleshooting such an issue would involve physically inspecting the cable to locate the break and then repairing or replacing the damaged section. Another example, though less common today, might be found in some older industrial control systems. While the bus topology might have been used in the past for its simplicity, modern industrial networks typically employ more robust topologies like star or ring to ensure higher reliability and fault tolerance. Therefore, while the bus topology offers simplicity in its basic implementation, its inherent vulnerability to cable breaks and performance limitations due to collisions have made it less suitable for most modern networking needs. Its historical significance lies in its role in the early development of networking technologies, but its use in contemporary networks is rare due to the availability of more reliable and scalable alternatives.

6.1.3 Ring Topology

The ring topology, a network architecture where devices are connected in a closed loop or ring, represents a distinct approach to network communication. In this configuration, each device connects to exactly two other devices, forming a continuous circular path for data transmission. Data travels around the ring, hopping from one device to the next, until it reaches its intended destination. Unlike the bus topology, where data is broadcast to all devices, in a ring topology, data travels in a specific direction. While offering some advantages in terms of performance under certain conditions, the ring topology, like the bus topology, has become less common in modern network deployments due to its inherent vulnerabilities and complexities. A key characteristic of the ring topology is that a break in the ring, whether due to a cable cut or a device failure, can disrupt communication for the entire network. Because data travels along a single path, a break anywhere in the ring can prevent data from reaching its destination. This single point of failure makes the ring topology less desirable for mission-critical applications where high availability is essential. As Kurose and Ross (2017) explain, "The primary disadvantage of the ring topology is its susceptibility to single points of failure" (p. 161). This vulnerability has been a major factor in its decline. A historical example of the ring topology is Token Ring networks, which were popular in the past, particularly in IBM environments. Token Ring networks used a "token" to control access to the network. Only the device holding the token was allowed to transmit data, preventing collisions that could occur in other topologies. However, the complexity of token management and the vulnerability to ring breaks contributed to the decline of Token Ring in favor of more robust and scalable topologies. Consider a manufacturing plant using a ring topology to connect various machines and control systems. A cable cut in the ring could halt production, as the control signals might not be able to reach the machines, highlighting the critical need for redundancy in such environments. Troubleshooting a ring network often involves isolating the break in the ring, which can be a time-consuming process. Another example, though less common now, might be found in some older industrial automation systems. While the ring topology might have been considered for its controlled access method, modern industrial networks typically employ more resilient topologies like star or mesh to ensure continuous operation. Therefore, while the ring topology offered some advantages in terms of controlled access and potentially higher performance under certain conditions, its vulnerability to single points of failure and the complexity of managing token passing (in the case of Token Ring) have made it less suitable for most modern networking needs. The rise of more reliable and scalable topologies, like the star topology, has led to the decline of the ring topology in contemporary network deployments.

6.2 NETWORK DEVICES

Several devices are essential for building and maintaining a network.

6.2.1 Routers

Routers are fundamental network devices that act as intelligent traffic directors, connecting different networks together and strategically routing data packets between them. They serve as gateways, enabling communication between distinct networks, such as a local home network and the vast expanse of the internet. Unlike switches, which operate at Layer 2 (Data Link Layer) of the OSI model and manage traffic within a single network, routers function at Layer 3 (Network Layer) and handle communication *between* networks. Their primary responsibility is to determine the most efficient path for data packets to traverse, ensuring they reach their intended destination across potentially multiple interconnected networks. Routers achieve this through the use of routing protocols, complex algorithms that analyze network topology and available paths to make informed routing decisions. These protocols, like OSPF (Open Shortest Path First) or BGP (Border Gateway Protocol), dynamically adapt to network changes, such as link failures or congestion, to maintain optimal data flow. As Kurose and Ross (2017) explain, "Routers are key components of the Internet, responsible for forwarding packets between networks" (p. 325). This underscores their crucial role in enabling global internet connectivity. A real-world example that is immediately familiar to most users is the router in a home network. This device connects the home network, consisting of various devices like computers, smartphones, and smart TVs, to the internet provided by an internet service provider (ISP). The router receives data packets from these devices destined for various locations on the internet and uses its routing table, built using a routing protocol, to forward these packets along the appropriate path to reach their destinations. Conversely, it also receives data packets from the internet intended for devices on the home network and directs them to the correct device. Consider a large enterprise network connecting multiple branch offices to the headquarters. Routers at each branch office connect the local network to the wide area network (WAN) that links all the locations. The routers use routing protocols to exchange information about network topology and available paths, enabling them to forward traffic between branches and the headquarters efficiently. Another example is a large data center hosting numerous web servers. Routers play a critical role in distributing incoming traffic from the internet to the appropriate servers, ensuring that user requests are handled efficiently and that server load is balanced. They also manage outbound traffic from the servers to users across the globe. Therefore, understanding the function and configuration of routers is essential for anyone working with computer networks. They are the linchpins of internet connectivity and crucial for managing communication between different networks, from small home networks to complex enterprise infrastructures and the global internet itself.

6.2.2 Switches

Switches are essential network devices that connect devices *within* the same local area network (LAN), acting as intelligent traffic managers to improve network efficiency and performance. Unlike older devices like hubs, which simply broadcast incoming data to all connected devices, switches operate at Layer 2 (Data Link Layer) of the OSI model and learn the Media Access Control (MAC) addresses of connected devices. This MAC address learning allows the switch to create a table mapping MAC addresses to specific ports. When a data packet arrives at the switch, it examines the destination MAC address and forwards the packet *only* to the port connected to the intended recipient. This targeted forwarding significantly reduces network congestion and improves overall performance by preventing unnecessary traffic from reaching devices that are not the intended recipients. As Kurose and Ross (2017) explain, "Switches forward packets based on MAC addresses, providing dedicated connections between devices" (p. 332). This dedicated connection minimizes collisions and improves network throughput compared to older shared-medium technologies. A real-world example is a typical office network. Each computer, printer, and other network-enabled device connects to a central switch. When one computer sends data to another computer on the same network, the switch forwards the data packet directly to the recipient's port, preventing other devices from being burdened with unnecessary traffic. This dedicated connection ensures that each device has a dedicated pathway for communication, improving network efficiency and reducing the likelihood of collisions. Consider a scenario in a busy office where multiple employees are transferring large files, accessing network applications, and printing documents. A switch ensures that this traffic is managed efficiently, preventing network congestion and ensuring that each user's data reaches its intended destination without interference. Without a switch, and if a hub were used instead, all devices would share the same bandwidth, leading to significant slowdowns and potential collisions. Another example is a data center hosting numerous servers. Switches play a crucial role in managing the high volume of traffic between servers, ensuring that data is routed efficiently and that server performance is optimized. They also provide connectivity between different server racks and other network infrastructure components. Therefore, understanding the function and configuration of switches is essential for anyone working with computer networks. They are the backbone of modern LANs, providing the intelligent traffic management necessary for efficient and reliable network communication. Their ability to learn MAC addresses and forward data packets only to the intended recipient significantly improves network performance and reduces congestion, making them indispensable in a wide range of networking environments.

6.2.3 Modems

Modems, short for modulator-demodulator, serve as crucial communication devices that bridge the gap between the digital world of computers and the analog world of traditional telecommunications infrastructure. Their primary function is to modulate and demodulate signals, enabling devices like computers to connect to the internet through cable or DSL (Digital Subscriber Line) connections. Modulation involves converting digital data from the computer into analog signals suitable for transmission over the telephone or cable line. This process essentially encodes the digital information into analog waveforms that can travel over these traditional communication mediums. Demodulation, conversely, is the reverse process, where the modem converts the incoming analog signals back into digital data that the computer can understand. This translation between digital and analog is the core function of the modem, allowing computers to communicate over infrastructure designed for analog signal transmission. As Kurose and Ross (2017) explain, "Modems are used to connect computers to analog transmission media, such as telephone lines or cable TV lines" (p. 345). This highlights their role as the interface between digital devices and analog communication channels. A real-world example is a home user connecting to the internet via a cable modem. The computer sends digital data, such as a request to view a web page, to the cable modem. The cable modem modulates this digital data into analog signals that can be transmitted over the cable line to the internet service provider (ISP). The ISP's equipment then receives these analog signals, demodulates them back into digital data, and routes the request to the appropriate web server. The web server's response follows the same process in reverse, with the cable modem demodulating the analog signals from the ISP back into digital data that the user's computer can interpret and display as the web page. Consider a small business using a DSL connection for internet access. The DSL modem at the office modulates and demodulates the digital data from the office network, enabling communication with the ISP over the existing telephone lines. This allows employees to access the internet, send emails, and use online services. Another example, though becoming less common with the rise of fiber optic connections, is a remote worker connecting to the internet through a dial-up modem. In this scenario, the dial-up modem modulates the digital data from the computer into analog audio signals that can be transmitted over the traditional telephone line. While dial-up connections are much slower than cable or DSL, they were historically significant in providing internet access to homes and businesses. Therefore, understanding the function of modems as modulators and demodulators is essential for anyone working with internet connectivity. They are the bridge between the digital and analog worlds, enabling computers to communicate over traditional telecommunications infrastructure. While newer technologies like fiber optic connections are increasingly replacing traditional cable and DSL, modems still play a role in many internet access scenarios.

6.3 BASIC NETWORKING CONCEPTS

Understanding basic networking concepts is essential for troubleshooting network issues.

6.3.1 IP Addresses

IP (Internet Protocol) addresses are fundamental numerical identifiers assigned to each device connected to a network, whether it's a local area network (LAN) or the vast expanse of the internet. They serve as unique identifiers, analogous to postal addresses for computers, enabling data packets to be routed to the correct destination. Just as a postal address distinguishes one house from another, an IP address distinguishes one device from another on the network, ensuring that data reaches the intended recipient. Two primary versions of IP addresses exist: IPv4 and IPv6. IPv4 addresses are 32-bit numerical identifiers, typically represented in dotted decimal notation (e.g., 192.168.1.1). While IPv4 has served as the backbone of internet addressing for many years, its limited address space (approximately 4.3 billion unique addresses) has become insufficient to accommodate the ever-growing number of internet-connected devices. IPv6 addresses, on the other hand, are 128-bit numerical identifiers, represented in hexadecimal notation (e.g., 2001:0db8:85a3:0000:0000:8a2e:0370:7334). This vastly expanded address space offers a virtually unlimited number of unique addresses, addressing the limitations of IPv4 and providing a foundation for future internet growth. As Kurose and Ross (2017) explain, "The IP address is the network layer address that is used to identify a host on the internet" (p. 405). This highlights the crucial role of IP addresses in internet communication. A real-world example that everyone experiences is accessing a website. When you type a website's domain name (e.g., www.example.com) into your browser, a Domain Name System (DNS) server translates that domain name into the corresponding IP address of the web server. Your computer then uses this IP address to send a request to the web server, and the server uses your computer's IP address to send the website's data back to you. Consider a large organization with a complex network infrastructure. Each device on the organization's network, from computers and printers to servers and network devices, is assigned a unique IP address. This allows network administrators to manage and monitor the network effectively, track device activity, and troubleshoot connectivity issues. Another example is a cloud computing environment where virtual machines (VMs) are constantly being created and destroyed. Each VM is assigned a unique IP address, allowing it to communicate with other VMs and external networks. The dynamic allocation of IP addresses in cloud environments is essential for scalability and efficient resource management. Therefore, understanding the structure and function of IP addresses, both IPv4 and IPv6, is fundamental for anyone working with computer networks. They are the foundation of internet communication, enabling devices to identify themselves and communicate with each other across local networks and the global internet. The transition from IPv4 to IPv6 is an ongoing process, driven by the need to accommodate the ever-expanding number of internet-connected devices and ensure the continued growth of the internet.

6.3.2 Subnets

Subnetting, a crucial concept in network administration, involves logically dividing a single physical network into multiple smaller, interconnected subnets. This subdivision allows for more efficient utilization of IP addresses, improved network performance, and enhanced security. Instead of assigning a large block of IP addresses to a single network, subnetting breaks down that block into smaller, more manageable chunks, allowing for a greater number of devices to be connected and a more organized network structure. Subnet masks, used in conjunction with IP addresses, define the boundaries of each subnet. They distinguish the network portion of the IP address from the host portion, enabling devices to determine whether they are on the same subnet or need to communicate through a router to reach another subnet. As Kurose and Ross (2017) explain, "Subnetting allows an organization to use a single network address prefix to create multiple physical networks" (p. 412). This efficient use of IP addresses is a key driver for subnetting. A common question is why subnetting is necessary. Several factors contribute to its importance. First, it helps to organize large networks, making them easier to manage and troubleshoot. Imagine a large organization with thousands of devices connected to a single network. Managing such a large, flat network would be incredibly complex. Subnetting breaks the network into smaller, more manageable units, such as departments or building floors, simplifying administration. Second, subnetting improves network performance by reducing network traffic. When devices communicate within the same subnet, the traffic remains local. Only traffic destined for other subnets or external networks needs to be routed, reducing congestion on the overall network. Third, subnetting enhances security by isolating different parts of the network. For example, sensitive data can be kept on a separate subnet, restricting access and limiting the impact of a security breach. Consider a university campus network. Subnetting might be used to separate student networks, faculty networks, and administrative networks. This isolation enhances security, preventing students from accessing sensitive administrative data and limiting the spread of malware if a student's computer becomes infected. Another real-world example is a data center hosting various applications and services. Subnetting allows for isolating different server groups based on their function or security requirements. For example, web servers might be on one subnet, database servers on another, and backup servers on a third.

This isolation improves security and simplifies network management. Therefore, understanding subnetting and its benefits is crucial for anyone managing computer networks, especially in larger or more complex environments. It's not just about using IP addresses efficiently; it's about organizing the network for better performance, enhanced security, and simplified administration.

6.4 WIRELESS NETWORKING

Wireless networking allows devices to connect to a network without physical cables.

6.4.1 Wi-Fi

Wi-Fi, short for Wireless Fidelity, has become the ubiquitous wireless networking technology, leveraging radio waves to transmit data between devices without the need for physical cables. Its widespread adoption in homes, offices, and public spaces has revolutionized how we connect to networks and access the internet. A Wi-Fi network requires a wireless access point (WAP) or, more commonly in home and small office settings, a combination router/WAP device. This device acts as the central hub for wireless communication, receiving data from connected devices and relaying it to the wired network or the internet. While offering convenience and mobility, Wi-Fi networks also present significant security concerns. Because radio waves are broadcast through the air, unauthorized individuals within range can potentially intercept network traffic or even gain access to the network. Therefore, implementing robust security measures is absolutely essential for protecting Wi-Fi networks from unauthorized access and malicious activity. Using strong and unique passwords for the Wi-Fi network is a foundational security practice. However, password strength alone is not sufficient. Enabling encryption protocols, such as WPA2 (Wi-Fi Protected Access 2) or the more recent WPA3, is crucial. These protocols encrypt the data transmitted over the Wi-Fi network, making it unreadable to anyone who might intercept the radio waves without the correct decryption key. As Kurose and Ross (2017) explain, "Security in wireless networks is a major concern due to the broadcast nature of radio transmissions" (p. 525). This vulnerability necessitates strong security measures. A common and dangerous misconception is that a Wi-Fi password alone is sufficient for security. While a strong password is important, other security measures are also crucial. Regularly updating the router's firmware is essential, as firmware updates often include security patches that address newly discovered vulnerabilities. Disabling WPS (Wi-Fi Protected Setup), a feature designed to simplify Wi-Fi setup, is also recommended if not needed. WPS has been shown to have security vulnerabilities that can be exploited to gain unauthorized access to the network. Consider a small business relying on Wi-Fi for its employees to connect to the network. Using a weak password or failing to enable WPA2/3 encryption could leave the network vulnerable to unauthorized access, potentially compromising sensitive business data. Regularly updating the router's firmware and disabling WPS would further strengthen the network's security. Another real-world example is a home user connecting various devices to their home Wi-Fi network. They might think that having a password is enough, but without WPA2/3 encryption, their neighbors or even individuals parked outside their house could potentially intercept their internet traffic or access their personal files. Therefore, understanding the security vulnerabilities of Wi-Fi networks and implementing a multi-layered security approach is vital for protecting data and privacy. It's not just about having a password; it's about using strong encryption protocols, regularly updating firmware, disabling WPS, and being aware of other potential security risks.

CHAPTER 7

CUSTOMER RELATIONS AND COMMUNICATION

In the realm of computer systems and technical support, possessing deep technical expertise is a fundamental requirement, but it's only one piece of the puzzle. Equally vital, and often underestimated, are strong customer relations and communication skills, particularly for technicians who interact directly with end-users. Technical prowess without the ability to effectively communicate with customers can lead to frustration, miscommunication, and ultimately, dissatisfied clients. This section explores the key aspects of effective communication in a technical context, delves into problem-solving strategies within a customer service framework, examines effective techniques for handling difficult or challenging customers, and underscores the importance of maintaining professionalism and adhering to ethical principles in all customer interactions. Consider a scenario where a technician is called to troubleshoot a network connectivity issue at a small business. Even if the technician quickly identifies the technical root cause, their ability to explain the problem in clear, non-technical language to the business owner, outlining the steps required for resolution and the potential impact on business operations, is crucial for building trust and managing expectations. Effective communication bridges the gap between technical expertise and user understanding. As Lewis (2017) points out, "Effective communication is essential for building rapport and trust with customers" (p. 125). This rapport is the foundation of positive customer relations. Another real-world example involves a help desk technician assisting a user with a software installation problem. The technician not only needs to guide the user through the process step-by-step but also needs to patiently listen to the user's concerns, address their questions, and provide clear instructions, even if the user is not technically savvy. A common challenge is dealing with difficult or irate customers. These situations require tact, empathy, and the ability to remain calm and professional under pressure. Active listening, acknowledging the customer's frustration, and focusing on finding a solution are key strategies for de-escalating tense situations. Consider a customer who has lost important data due to a hard drive failure. They might be understandably upset and stressed. The technician's ability to empathize with the customer's situation, explain the data recovery options clearly and honestly, and offer support throughout the process can make a significant difference in the customer's perception of the service, even if the data cannot be fully recovered. Furthermore, maintaining professionalism and adhering to ethical principles are paramount. Honesty, integrity, and respect for customer privacy are essential for building long-term customer relationships. Therefore, while technical skills are undoubtedly important, the ability to communicate effectively, solve problems in a customer-centric manner, handle difficult situations with grace, and uphold professional and ethical standards are equally crucial for success in the field of computer systems and technical support. These soft skills are not merely an added bonus; they are integral to providing excellent customer service and building a strong reputation.

7.1 EFFECTIVE COMMUNICATION SKILLS

Effective communication forms the cornerstone of positive customer interactions in the technical field. It's not simply about conveying information; it's about ensuring that the recipient understands the message clearly and completely. This involves a multifaceted approach, encompassing clear and concise verbal communication, active listening to fully grasp the customer's issue, and the ability to translate complex technical concepts into language accessible to non-technical users. Avoiding technical jargon, which can alienate and confuse customers, is paramount. Instead, using relatable analogies and everyday examples can significantly improve comprehension. For instance, instead of explaining RAM as "volatile memory," a technician might say, "RAM is like a whiteboard where the computer keeps information it's actively working on. When you turn off the computer, the whiteboard is erased." This analogy connects the technical concept to a familiar object, making it much easier for a non-technical user to understand. Non-verbal communication, often overlooked, plays a crucial role in building rapport and trust.

Maintaining appropriate eye contact, using open and welcoming body language, and employing a positive and encouraging tone of voice can convey empathy and build confidence in the customer. These non-verbal cues communicate attentiveness and a genuine desire to help. As Lewis (2017) states, "Effective communication involves both verbal and non-verbal cues" (p. 132). This highlights the importance of considering all aspects of communication. A common mistake technicians make is assuming the customer understands technical terminology. This assumption can lead to miscommunication, frustration, and ultimately, an unresolved problem. Adapting communication to the customer's level of understanding is absolutely essential for effective problem-solving. A technician should always assess the customer's technical background and tailor their explanations accordingly. If the customer is not technically inclined, the technician should use simple language, avoid jargon, and focus on explaining the problem and solution in terms of its impact on the customer's workflow or experience. Consider a scenario where a user is experiencing slow internet speeds. Instead of discussing technical details like bandwidth or latency, the technician might explain it as "like having a slow water pipe – it takes longer for the water (data) to reach you." This analogy makes the concept of limited bandwidth more understandable to a non-technical user. Another real-world example involves a technician explaining a software update to a user. Instead of using technical terms like "patch" or "vulnerability," the technician might explain it as "an important fix that helps keep your computer safe from problems." Therefore, effective communication in a technical context is about more than just technical knowledge; it's about the ability to connect with the customer on their level, explain complex concepts in simple terms, and build trust through both verbal and non-verbal communication. Adapting communication to the customer's understanding is the key to successful problem-solving and positive customer interactions.

7.2 PROBLEM-SOLVING AND CUSTOMER SERVICE

When a customer reports a technical problem, the technician's role extends beyond simply fixing the immediate issue; it encompasses providing excellent customer service throughout the entire interaction. This customer-centric approach is crucial for building trust, fostering positive relationships, and ensuring customer satisfaction. Effective problem-solving in a customer service context begins with active listening. Carefully attending to the customer's description of the problem, even if it seems vague or non-technical, is essential for gathering the necessary information. Asking clarifying questions is equally important. These questions should be designed to elicit specific details about the problem, such as when it started, what programs are affected, and any recent changes to the system. This systematic approach helps narrow down the potential causes and guides the troubleshooting process. Explaining the solution in a clear and understandable manner is vital. Technical jargon should be avoided, and the explanation should be tailored to the customer's level of technical understanding. Using analogies, diagrams, or step-by-step instructions can significantly improve comprehension. Empathy and patience are paramount, especially when dealing with frustrated or stressed customers. Acknowledging their frustration, actively listening to their concerns, and remaining calm and professional, even in challenging situations, can de-escalate tension and build rapport. As Reynolds (2019) notes, "Empathy is a critical component of effective customer service" (p. 87). This empathy allows technicians to connect with customers on a human level and build trust. Documenting the problem and the solution is crucial for future reference and knowledge sharing. This documentation can be used to create a knowledge base, train other technicians, and prevent similar problems from recurring. A real-world scenario might involve a user reporting a slow computer. Instead of immediately resorting to drastic measures like reinstalling the operating system, a skilled technician should first ask clarifying questions. "When did the problem start?" "What programs are running when the computer slows down?" "Have you installed any new software or hardware recently?" These questions can help pinpoint the root cause, which might be a software conflict, a failing hard drive, or simply too many programs running at startup. Consider a user reporting that their email program is not sending messages. Instead of assuming it's a problem with the email server, the technician should first ask questions like, "Are you receiving error messages?" "Can you access your email through a web browser?" "Have you changed your email password recently?" These questions can help determine if the issue is with the email client, the server, or a configuration problem. Therefore, effective problem-solving in a customer service context involves not only technical expertise but also strong communication skills, empathy, patience, and a systematic approach to gathering information, diagnosing problems, and explaining solutions. Documenting these interactions is essential for continuous improvement and providing consistent, high-quality service.

7.3 HANDLING DIFFICULT CUSTOMERS

Interacting with customers in a technical support role is not always a smooth experience. Technicians will inevitably encounter difficult customers who may be angry, impatient, or even unreasonable. The ability to navigate these challenging interactions effectively is a crucial skill, distinguishing a competent technician from an exceptional one. Remaining calm and professional, even under pressure, is paramount. Reacting emotionally or defensively will only escalate the situation. Active listening, demonstrating genuine empathy for the customer's frustration, and expressing a willingness to help are key strategies for diffusing tension. Acknowledging the customer's feelings, even if you don't agree with their assessment of the situation, can go a long way in de-escalating the interaction. Avoid taking things personally; remember that the customer's frustration is likely directed at the situation, not at you as an individual. If the customer becomes abusive, threatening, or engages in personal attacks, it's important to set boundaries politely but firmly. Explain that while you are willing to help resolve their technical issue, you cannot tolerate abusive behavior. If the behavior continues, it's essential to escalate the issue to a supervisor or manager. As Reynolds (2019) advises, "Setting boundaries is essential for protecting yourself and maintaining professionalism" (p. 102). This self-protection allows technicians to remain effective in their roles. A common challenge is dealing with customers who have unrealistic expectations. This can stem from a lack of understanding about the technology, a miscommunication about the scope of the service, or simply a desire for an immediate fix, regardless of the complexity of the problem. Clearly explaining the limitations of the technology and setting realistic expectations upfront is essential for managing these situations. For example, a customer might expect a complex computer repair to be completed within an hour, even though the problem requires extensive troubleshooting and parts may need to be ordered. Clearly communicating the estimated timeframe, explaining the reasons for any potential delays, and providing regular updates can help manage expectations and prevent frustration. Consider a customer who is extremely upset because their website is down. While acknowledging their frustration, the technician should explain the troubleshooting process, outlining the steps they are taking to diagnose the problem and providing an estimated time for resolution. Keeping the customer informed throughout the process can help alleviate their anxiety. Another real-world example involves a user who is demanding a refund for a software application that is not working as expected. The technician should listen to the user's complaint, attempt to troubleshoot the issue, and, if the problem cannot be resolved, explain the company's refund policy clearly and professionally, even if the policy is not what the customer wants to hear. Therefore, handling difficult customers effectively requires a combination of technical expertise, strong communication skills, empathy, patience, and the ability to set boundaries. By remaining calm, professional, and focused on finding a solution, technicians can navigate these challenging interactions and maintain positive customer relationships.

7.4 PROFESSIONALISM AND ETHICS

Professionalism and ethics are not merely desirable qualities in the field of computer systems and technical support; they are foundational pillars upon which trust is built and a positive reputation is established. These principles guide behavior, shape interactions, and ultimately define the character of a professional. Professionalism encompasses a range of qualities, including punctuality in appointments and meetings, appropriate attire that reflects the context of the work environment, and respectful communication with customers, colleagues, and supervisors. It's about presenting oneself in a manner that inspires confidence and demonstrates competence. Ethics, on the other hand, delve into moral principles that govern conduct and decision-making. Respecting customer privacy is paramount, particularly when dealing with sensitive data, whether it's personal information, financial records, or confidential business documents. Maintaining confidentiality is not just a matter of courtesy; it's a legal and ethical obligation. Acting with integrity, being honest and transparent in all interactions, and adhering to a code of ethics are crucial for maintaining trust and upholding professional standards. As the CompTIA Code of Professional Ethics (CompTIA, n.d.) articulates, "IT professionals shall act with integrity and maintain the highest standards of competence." This code provides a framework for ethical decision-making, guiding professionals in navigating complex situations and resolving ethical dilemmas. A real-world ethical dilemma might involve a technician discovering unlicensed or illegal software on a customer's computer during a service call. The technician has a responsibility to address this issue, which might involve informing the customer about the legal implications of using unlicensed software and, in some cases, reporting the issue to the appropriate authorities, particularly if the software use poses a security risk to others. This situation highlights the tension between customer service and ethical obligations. A common question is how to balance these competing demands. While providing excellent customer service is undoubtedly important, it should never come at the expense of ethical principles. Ethical obligations must take precedence. Consider a scenario where a technician is asked by a customer to perform a task that they know is unethical or illegal, such as bypassing security measures or accessing confidential data without authorization. The technician has a clear ethical obligation to refuse to perform the task, even if it means potentially losing the customer. Explaining the ethical and legal implications of the request to the customer can be a constructive approach. Another example involves a technician who discovers a security vulnerability in a customer's system. While fixing the vulnerability might be a simple technical task, the technician also has an ethical obligation to inform the customer about the vulnerability and explain the potential risks, even if the customer is not aware of it or chooses not to address it. Therefore, professionalism and ethics are not just abstract concepts; they are practical guidelines that shape behavior and inform decision-making in the field of computer systems and technical support. Adhering to a code of ethics, maintaining confidentiality, acting with integrity, and balancing customer service with ethical obligations are all essential for building trust, maintaining a positive reputation, and upholding the highest standards of professional conduct.

CHAPTER 8

ADVANCED TOPICS

As computer systems become increasingly complex, technicians and IT professionals often need to delve into more advanced concepts. This optional section introduces three key areas: virtualization, cloud computing, and scripting/automation. While not strictly required for basic computer repair, familiarity with these topics provides a significant advantage in today's IT landscape.

8.1 INTRODUCTION TO VIRTUALIZATION

Virtualization has become a cornerstone of modern computing, enabling the creation and management of multiple virtual machines (VMs) on a single physical machine. This powerful technology allows each VM to operate as if it were a separate physical computer, complete with its own operating system, applications, and allocated resources, all isolated from other VMs running on the same physical hardware. This isolation is a key benefit, preventing issues within one VM from affecting others and providing a secure environment for running different applications or operating systems concurrently. The advantages of virtualization are numerous, including significantly improved resource utilization, reduced hardware costs due to server consolidation, simplified management through centralized control, and increased flexibility in deploying and managing applications. Hypervisors, specialized software or firmware, are the engine behind virtualization, responsible for creating, managing, and allocating resources to the VMs. Popular hypervisors include VMware vSphere, Microsoft Hyper-V, and KVM (Kernel-based Virtual Machine), each with its own features and capabilities. As Buyya et al. (2016) explain, "Virtualization is a technique for abstracting the physical resources of a computer into several logical resources" (p. 2). This abstraction is what makes virtualization so powerful and flexible. A real-world scenario illustrating the benefits of virtualization involves a company consolidating multiple physical servers into a smaller number of more powerful physical machines. By running these server applications as VMs on the consolidated hardware, the company can significantly reduce hardware costs, power consumption, and cooling requirements, leading to substantial operational savings. Another common use case is in software development. Developers can leverage VMs to test their code in different operating system environments and configurations without needing separate physical machines for each environment. This accelerates the testing process and reduces the overhead of managing multiple physical test machines. A common question that arises when discussing virtualization is how it differs from emulation. While both virtualization and emulation involve running one system on another, they operate on fundamentally different principles. Virtualization utilizes the host's physical resources directly, allowing VMs to achieve near-native performance. The hypervisor acts as a thin layer between the VMs and the hardware, efficiently allocating resources as needed. Emulation, on the other hand, simulates the hardware of one system on another. This simulation is computationally intensive and typically leads to significantly slower performance compared to virtualization. Imagine trying to run a modern video game on a computer emulating a much older gaming console. The emulation process would likely result in poor performance and unplayable frame rates. Virtualization, in contrast, would allow the same game to run smoothly on a VM with access to the host's powerful hardware. Therefore, understanding the principles of virtualization, its benefits, and its distinction from emulation is crucial for anyone working in modern IT environments. From server consolidation and software development to cloud computing and disaster recovery, virtualization has become an indispensable technology, offering efficiency, flexibility, and cost savings.

8.2 Cloud Computing Basics

Cloud computing has revolutionized the way organizations and individuals access and utilize computing resources. It involves delivering a wide array of computing services—encompassing servers, storage, databases, networking, software, analytics, and even artificial intelligence—over the internet, often referred to as "the cloud." Instead of owning and maintaining their own often expensive and complex IT infrastructure, organizations can access these resources on demand from cloud providers, such as Amazon Web Services (AWS), Microsoft Azure, and Google Cloud Platform (GCP). This on-demand access offers several key advantages, including scalability, allowing resources to be easily increased or decreased as needed; flexibility, providing access to a diverse range of services and tools; and cost-effectiveness, eliminating the need for large upfront capital investments in hardware and infrastructure. As Mell and Grance (2011) define it, "Cloud computing is a model for enabling ubiquitous, convenient, on-demand network access to a shared pool of configurable computing resources (e.g., networks, servers, storage, applications, and services) that can be rapidly provisioned and

189

released with minimal management effort or service provider interaction." This[1] definition highlights the key characteristics of cloud computing. A real-world example illustrating the benefits of cloud computing is a startup company using cloud storage to store its data. This eliminates the need for the company to invest in and manage expensive storage hardware, such as hard drives or tape libraries. Cloud storage also provides automatic scalability, meaning that the storage capacity can be easily increased as the company's data grows, without requiring any manual intervention. Another common use case is running web applications in the cloud. Cloud platforms allow for automatic scaling of resources, such as server capacity, based on traffic demand. If the website experiences a sudden surge in visitors, the cloud platform can automatically provision additional servers to handle the increased load, ensuring that the website remains responsive and available. A common question that arises when discussing cloud computing is the different types of cloud computing services available. These services are typically categorized into three main models: Infrastructure as a Service (IaaS), Platform as a Service (PaaS), and Software as a Service (SaaS). IaaS provides access to fundamental computing resources, such as virtual servers, storage, and networking. It offers a high degree of control and flexibility, allowing users to configure and manage their own infrastructure. PaaS provides a platform for developing, deploying, and managing applications. It offers tools and services for building, testing, and deploying applications without the need to manage the underlying infrastructure. SaaS provides access to ready-to-use software applications over the internet. Users can access these applications on demand, without needing to install or manage them on their own devices. Consider a software development company. They might use IaaS to host their development and testing environments, PaaS to deploy and manage their web applications, and SaaS for tools like email and collaboration software. Therefore, understanding the basics of cloud computing and the different service models (IaaS, PaaS, SaaS) is essential for anyone working in modern IT environments. Cloud computing has transformed the way organizations consume IT resources, offering scalability, flexibility, and cost-effectiveness, and it has become a fundamental part of the IT landscape.

8.3 SCRIPTING AND AUTOMATION (POWERSHELL, BASH)

Scripting and automation have become indispensable skills for IT professionals, enabling them to automate repetitive tasks, manage systems efficiently, and streamline complex workflows. These skills are essential for maximizing productivity, minimizing human error, and ensuring consistent system operation. PowerShell, a powerful scripting language developed by Microsoft, is the primary tool for automation in Windows environments. Its deep integration with the Windows operating system and its extensive set of cmdlets (pre-built commands) allow administrators to automate virtually any aspect of Windows system administration, from user account management and software deployment to network configuration and system monitoring. Bash, a scripting language commonly used in Linux and macOS environments, is equally crucial for automating tasks in these Unix-like operating systems. Its versatility and powerful command-line tools make it ideal for automating system administration, file manipulation, and application deployment. As Beattie et al. (2017) explain, "Scripting languages are essential for automating system administration tasks" (p. 156). This highlights the critical role scripting plays in modern IT operations. A real-world scenario illustrating the benefits of scripting involves a system administrator using a PowerShell script to automate the process of creating user accounts on a Windows server. Instead of manually creating each account through a graphical interface, the administrator can write a script that automates the process, including setting user passwords, assigning group memberships, and configuring user profiles. This not only saves significant time but also reduces the risk of human error compared to manual account creation. Another use case is using a Bash script to automate the process of backing up files on a Linux server. The script can be scheduled to run regularly, automatically backing up critical data to a designated storage location. This ensures that backups are performed consistently and reliably, protecting against data loss due to hardware failure or other unforeseen events. A common question is which scripting language to learn. While the specific choice often depends on the target environment, PowerShell is generally preferred for Windows environments due to its tight integration with the Windows ecosystem. Bash, on the other hand, is the dominant scripting language in Linux and macOS environments.

193

Learning both languages provides a broader skillset and allows technicians to work effectively in diverse IT environments. Consider a large organization with a mixed IT infrastructure, including both Windows and Linux servers. IT professionals in this environment would benefit from knowing both PowerShell and Bash to manage the different systems effectively. They might use PowerShell to automate tasks on Windows servers and Bash to automate tasks on Linux servers. Another example is a DevOps engineer using scripting to automate the deployment of applications to cloud platforms. They might use a combination of Bash and other scripting languages to automate the entire deployment pipeline, from building the application to deploying it to the cloud and configuring the necessary infrastructure. Therefore, mastering scripting and automation with tools like PowerShell and Bash is an essential skill for any IT professional. It enables them to automate repetitive tasks, manage systems efficiently, and streamline complex workflows, ultimately improving productivity and ensuring consistent system operation.

Definition of Terms

1. **Adapter Card** – A hardware component inserted into a motherboard slot to add functionality, such as graphics, sound, or network capabilities.

2. **Anti-Static Wrist Strap** – A safety device used to prevent electrostatic discharge (ESD) when handling electronic components.

3. **Application Software** – Programs designed to perform specific tasks for users, such as word processing or web browsing.

4. **Basic Input/Output System (BIOS)** – Firmware that initializes hardware and manages the boot process of a computer.

5. **Cache Memory** – A small, high-speed memory storage located near the CPU to improve processing speed.

6. **Central Processing Unit (CPU)** – The main processing unit of a computer that executes instructions and performs calculations.

7. **Chipset** – A set of integrated circuits on the motherboard that manage communication between hardware components.

8. **Cloud Computing** – A computing model where resources and services are accessed remotely via the internet.

9. **Computer Architecture** – The design and organization of a computer's hardware and system components.

10. **Computer Network** – A system of interconnected devices that communicate and share resources.

11. **Computer System** – A combination of hardware, software, and firmware that processes data and performs tasks.

12. **Cooling System** – A mechanism, including fans and liquid cooling, used to prevent computer components from overheating.

13. **Data Flow Diagram (DFD)** – A graphical representation of how data moves within a system.

14. **Device Driver** – Software that enables an operating system to communicate with hardware components.

15. **Digital Storage** – Devices that retain data in digital form, such as SSDs, HDDs, and cloud storage.

16. **Electrostatic Discharge (ESD)** – The sudden flow of electricity between two charged objects, which can damage electronic components.

17. **Embedded System** – A specialized computing system integrated into a larger device to perform dedicated functions.

18. **Ethernet** – A widely used wired networking technology for local area networks (LANs).

19. **Expansion Slot** – A socket on a motherboard used for adding adapter cards to extend a computer's functionality.

20. **Firmware** – Low-level software embedded in hardware that provides control and communication between system components.

21. **Form Factor** – The physical dimensions and layout of hardware components, such as motherboards or cases.

22. **Graphics Processing Unit (GPU)** – A specialized processor designed to handle rendering and graphical computations.

23. **Hard Disk Drive (HDD)** – A mechanical storage device that uses spinning platters to store data persistently.

24. **Heat Sink** – A passive cooling device attached to a component to dissipate heat and prevent overheating.

25. **Input/Output (I/O) Devices** – Peripherals that allow users to interact with a computer, such as keyboards, mice, and monitors.

26. **Internet of Things (IoT)** – A network of interconnected devices that communicate and exchange data over the internet.

27. **Kernel** – The core component of an operating system that manages system resources and hardware interactions.

28. **Laptop** – A portable computer that integrates all components, including display, keyboard, and battery, in a single unit.

29. **Liquid Cooling** – A cooling system that uses liquid-based thermal transfer to regulate computer component temperatures.

30. **Local Area Network (LAN)** – A network that connects devices within a limited geographical area, such as an office or home.

31. **Memory (RAM)** – Temporary storage that holds data and programs actively used by the CPU for faster access.

32. **Motherboard** – The main circuit board that connects and facilitates communication between all computer components.

33. **Multimeter** – A diagnostic tool used to measure voltage, current, and resistance in electronic circuits.

34. **Network Interface Card (NIC)** – A hardware component that connects a computer to a network, enabling communication.

35. **Non-Volatile Memory Express (NVMe)** – A high-speed storage protocol designed to improve SSD performance over PCIe connections.

36. **Operating System (OS)** – System software that manages hardware and software resources, providing a user interface.

37. **Optical Drive** – A device that reads and writes data from optical discs such as CDs, DVDs, and Blu-ray discs.

38. **Overclocking** – The process of increasing a CPU or GPU's clock speed beyond factory settings for higher performance.

39. **Peripheral Device** – External hardware, such as printers or external hard drives, that connects to a computer to extend functionality.

40. **Personal Computer (PC)** – A general-purpose computer designed for individual use.

41. **Power Supply Unit (PSU)** – The component that converts electrical power from an outlet into usable power for a computer.

42. **Printer** – An output device that produces a hard copy of digital documents and images.

43. **Process Scheduler** – A system function that manages task execution and resource allocation in an operating system.

44. **Processor Core** – A unit within a CPU capable of executing instructions independently. Modern CPUs have multiple cores for parallel processing.

45. **Protocol** – A set of rules that define how data is transmitted and received over a network.

46. **Random Access Memory (RAM)** – A type of volatile memory that temporarily stores data for quick access by the CPU.

47. **Solid-State Drive (SSD)** – A fast, non-mechanical storage device that uses flash memory to store data.

48. **System Unit** – The main body of a computer, housing the motherboard, CPU, RAM, storage, and power supply.

REFERENCES

1. Beattie, M., Sayers, M. P., & Wheeler, D. J. (2017). Professional Linux system administration. John Wiley & Sons.

2. Buyya, R., Yeo, C. S., Venugopal, S., Broberg, J., & Brandic, I. (2016). Cloud computing and emerging IT platforms: Vision, hype, and reality for delivering computing as the 5th utility. Morgan Kaufmann.

3. CompTIA. (n.d.). CompTIA code of professional ethics. Retrieved from [CompTIA Website - Insert Actual Link Here]

4. Horowitz, P., & Hill, W. (2015). The art of electronics (3rd ed.). Cambridge University Press.

5. Kurose, J. F., & Ross, K. W. (2017). Computer networking: A top-down approach (7th ed.). Pearson.

6. Lewis, D. (2017). The customer service handbook. Kogan Page Publishers.

7. Mell, P., & Grance, T. (2011). The NIST definition of cloud computing. National Institute of Standards and Technology.

8. Mueller, S. (2017). Upgrading and repairing PCs (22nd ed.). Pearson.

9. Reynolds, S. (2019). Customer service: Skills for success. McGraw-Hill Education.

This page is intentionally left blank.

ABOUT THE AUTHOR

Mark John Lado is an accomplished Information System Specialist with a strong background in education and technology. He holds a Master's degree in Information Technology from Northern Negros State College of Science and Technology and is currently pursuing his Doctorate in the same field.

Mark boasts a diverse professional experience, having served as an ICT Instructor/Coordinator at Carmen Christian School Inc., a Part-time Information Technology Instructor at the University of the Visayas, and a Faculty member at Colegio de San Antonio de Padua and Cebu Technological University. He is currently a Faculty member at the College of Technology and Engineering at Cebu Technological University.

His expertise extends beyond the classroom, encompassing Object-Oriented Programming, Teacher Mentoring, Computer Hardware,

Software System Analysis, and Web Development. He actively participates in the Philippine Society of Information Technology Educators (PSITE) as a member and has contributed to the academic community through the publication of his research article, "A Wireless Digital Public Address with Voice Alarm and Text-to-speech Feature for Different Campuses," in Globus An International Journal of Management & IT.

Mark's dedication to education and passion for technology are evident in his contributions to various educational institutions, including Cebu Technological University, University of the Visayas - Danao Campus, Colegio de San Antonio de Padua, and Carmen Christian School Inc.

Biography Source:

Mark John Lado. (n.d.). *Biographies.net.* Retrieved January 24, 2025, from https://www.biographies.net/

Authors' Official Website:

https://markjohnlado.com/

This page is intentionally left blank.

www.ingramcontent.com/pod-product-compliance
Lightning Source LLC
LaVergne TN
LVHW022341060326
832902LV00022B/4179